Java 9 Dependency Injection

Write loosely coupled code with Spring 5 and Guice

Krunal Patel
Nilang Patel

BIRMINGHAM - MUMBAI

Java 9 Dependency Injection

Commissioning Editor: Merint Mathew
Acquisition Editors: Denim Pinto / Nitin Dasan
Content Development Editor: Anugraha Arunagiri
Technical Editor: Jijo Maliyekal
Copy Editor: Safis Editing
Project Coordinator: Ulhas Kambali
Proofreader: Safis Editing
Indexer: Rekha Nair
Graphics: Tania Dutta
Production Coordinator: Arvindkumar Gupta

First published: April 2018

Production reference: 1250418

Published by Packt Publishing Ltd.
Livery Place
35 Livery Street
Birmingham
B3 2PB, UK.

ISBN 978-1-78829-625-0

www.packtpub.com

`mapt.io`

Mapt is an online digital library that gives you full access to over 5,000 books and videos, as well as industry leading tools to help you plan your personal development and advance your career. For more information, please visit our website.

Why subscribe?

- Spend less time learning and more time coding with practical eBooks and Videos from over 4,000 industry professionals

- Improve your learning with Skill Plans built especially for you

- Get a free eBook or video every month

- Mapt is fully searchable

- Copy and paste, print, and bookmark content

PacktPub.com

Did you know that Packt offers eBook versions of every book published, with PDF and ePub files available? You can upgrade to the eBook version at `www.PacktPub.com` and as a print book customer, you are entitled to a discount on the eBook copy. Get in touch with us at `service@packt.pub.com` for more details.

At `www.PacktPub.com`, you can also read a collection of free technical articles, sign up for a range of free newsletters, and receive exclusive discounts and offers on Packt books and eBooks.

Contributors

About the authors

Krunal Patel has been working at Liferay Portal for over 5 years and has over 9 years of experience in enterprise application development using Java and Java EE technologies. He has worked in various domains, such as healthcare, hospitality, and enterprise intranet.

He was awarded an ITIL® Foundation Certificate in IT Service Management in 2015, a Liferay 6.1 Developer Certification in 2013, and a MongoDB for Java Developers certificate in 2013.

He has reviewed *Mastering Apache Solr 7.x* by Packt Publishing.

> *I would like to thank my loving wife Jigna, son Dirgh, father Maheshbhai, mother Sudhaben, brother Niraj, sister-in-law Krishna, and niece Risha, for supporting me throughout the course of writing this book. Thanks also to KNOWARTH, my coauthor and the Packt team, especially Anugraha and Peter Verhas, for their insightful comments.*

Nilang Patel has over 14 years of core IT experience in leading project, software design and development, and supporting enterprise applications using enterprise Java technologies.

He is experienced in core Java/J2EE based application and has experience in healthcare, human resource, taxation, intranet application, energy and risk management domain. He contributes to various forums and has a personal blog.

He acquired the Liferay 6.1 Developer Certification in 2013, Brainbench Java 6 certification in 2012, and a Sun Certified Programmer for the Java 2 Platform 1.5 (SCJP) in 2007.

> *With the divine blessings of Bhagwan Swaminarayan and my guru HH Pramukh Swami Maharaj and Mahant Swami Maharaj, I, Nilang could accomplish such a wonderful milestone. I am equally thankful to all reviewers at Packt. I would like to express my deep gratitude to my wife Komal and my daughters Bhakti and Harmi for making all possible adjustments and for their support.*

About the reviewer

Peter Verhas is a senior software engineer and software architect with a background in electrical engineering and economics. He gained an MSc from TU Budapest and an MBA from PTE Hungary, and studied at TU Delft and TU Vienna too. He created his first programs in 1979, and since then, he has authored several open source programs.

Peter now works for EPAM Systems in Switzerland, participating in software development projects at various customer sites. He also supports talent acquisition, interviewing candidates, and designing internal mentoring and training programs for developers.

Packt is searching for authors like you

If you're interested in becoming an author for Packt, please visit authors.packtpub.com and apply today. We have worked with thousands of developers and tech professionals, just like you, to help them share their insight with the global tech community. You can make a general application, apply for a specific hot topic that we are recruiting an author for, or submit your own idea.

Table of Contents

Preface

Dependency Injection is a design pattern that allows us to remove the hardcoded dependencies and make our application loosely coupled, extendable, and maintainable. We can implement dependency injection to move the dependency resolution from compile-time to runtime.

This book will be your one-stop guide to writing loosely coupled code using the latest features of Java 9 with frameworks such as Spring 5 and Google Guice.

Who this book is for

This book is for Java developers who would like to understand how to implement Dependency Injection in their applications. Prior knowledge about the Spring and Guice frameworks and Java programming is assumed.

What this book covers

Chapter 1, *Why Dependency Injection?*, gives you a detailed insight into various concepts, such as Dependency Inversion of Principle (DIP), Inversion of Control (IoC), and Dependency Injection (DI). It also talks about practical use cases where DI is commonly used.

Chapter 2, *Dependency Injection in Java 9*, gets you acquainted with Java 9 features and its modular framework, and explains how to implement DI using the service loader concept.

Chapter 3, *Dependency Injection with Spring*, teaches you how to manage dependency injection in the Spring framework. It also describes a different way to implement DI using Spring.

Chapter 4, *Dependency Injection with Google Guice*, talks about Guice and its dependency mechanism, and it teaches us dependency binding and the various injection methods of the Guice framework.

Chapter 5, *Scopes*, teaches you about the different scopes defined in the Spring and Guice frameworks.

Chapter 6, *Aspect-Oriented Programming and Interceptors*, shows the purpose of Aspect-Oriented Programming (AOP), how it solves different design problems by isolating repeated code from applications and plug them dynamically using Spring framework.

Chapter 7, *IoC Patterns and Best Practices*, gives an overview of various design patterns that can use to achieve IoC. Apart from this, you will be acquainted with best practices and anti-patterns to follow while injecting DI.

To get the most out of this book

1. It would be good if you know Java, Spring, and the Guice framework. This will help you understand dependency injection
2. We assume you have an installation of Java 9, and Maven on your system, before beginning

Download the example code files

You can download the example code files for this book from your account at www.packtpub.com. If you purchased this book elsewhere, you can visit www.packtpub.com/support and register to have the files emailed directly to you.

You can download the code files by following these steps:

1. Log in or register at www.packtpub.com.
2. Select the **SUPPORT** tab.
3. Click on **Code Downloads & Errata**.
4. Enter the name of the book in the **Search** box and follow the onscreen instructions.

Once the file is downloaded, please make sure that you unzip or extract the folder using the latest version of:

- WinRAR/7-Zip for Windows
- Zipeg/iZip/UnRarX for Mac
- 7-Zip/PeaZip for Linux

The code bundle for the book is also hosted on GitHub at `https://github.com/PacktPublishing/Java-9-Dependency-Injection`. We also have other code bundles from our rich catalog of books and videos available at `https://github.com/PacktPublishing/`. Check them out!

Download the color images

We also provide a PDF file that has color images of the screenshots/diagrams used in this book. You can download it here: `https://www.packtpub.com/sites/default/files/downloads/Java9DependencyInjection_ColorImages.pdf`.

Conventions used

There are a number of text conventions used throughout this book.

`CodeInText`: Indicates code words in text, database table names, folder names, filenames, file extensions, pathnames, dummy URLs, user input, and Twitter handles. Here is an example: "Mount the downloaded `WebStorm-10*.dmg` disk image file as another disk on your system."

A block of code is set as follows:

```
module javaIntroduction {
}
```

Any command-line input or output is written as follows:

```
$ mkdir css
$ cd css
```

Bold: Indicates a new term, an important word, or words that you see onscreen. For example, words in menus or dialog boxes appear in the text like this. Here is an example: "Select **System info** from the **Administration** panel."

Warnings or important notes appear like this.

Tips and tricks appear like this.

Get in touch

Feedback from our readers is always welcome.

General feedback: Email `feedback@packtpub.com` and mention the book title in the subject of your message. If you have questions about any aspect of this book, please email us at `questions@packtpub.com`.

Errata: Although we have taken every care to ensure the accuracy of our content, mistakes do happen. If you have found a mistake in this book, we would be grateful if you would report this to us. Please visit `www.packtpub.com/submit-errata`, selecting your book, clicking on the Errata Submission Form link, and entering the details.

Piracy: If you come across any illegal copies of our works in any form on the Internet, we would be grateful if you would provide us with the location address or website name. Please contact us at `copyright@packtpub.com` with a link to the material.

If you are interested in becoming an author: If there is a topic that you have expertise in and you are interested in either writing or contributing to a book, please visit `authors.packtpub.com`.

Reviews

Please leave a review. Once you have read and used this book, why not leave a review on the site that you purchased it from? Potential readers can then see and use your unbiased opinion to make purchase decisions, we at Packt can understand what you think about our products, and our authors can see your feedback on their book. Thank you!

For more information about Packt, please visit `packtpub.com`.

Why Dependency Injection?

In software development, very often someone else might already have found effective solutions to the problems you are facing.

As a developer, you don't need to reinvent the wheel every time. Instead, you need to refer to the well-established practices and methodologies. Have you guessed what we are talking about? That's correct: *design patterns*.

This chapter is crafted to cover the following interesting topics:

- What design patterns are and their benefits
- **Dependency Injection Principle (DIP)**
- **Inversion of Control (IoC)**—a design methodology to implement DIP
- Various design patterns to implement IoC
- **Dependency Injection (DI)**
- Various types to implement DI
- How an IoC container is helpful to apply a DI

Design patterns

By definition, a **design pattern** is a set of proven de facto industry standards and best practices for resolving recurring problems. Design patterns are not ready-made solutions. Rather, they're a way or template to implement and apply the best possible solution for your problem.

It's equally true that if a design pattern is not implemented in the right way, it creates a lot of problems rather than solving the one you expected to solve. So it's very important to know which design pattern, if any, is right for a specific scenario.

Design patterns are a common paradigm to describe the problem and how to solve it. It's usually not language specific. Design patterns can protect you from the design problems that generally occur in the later stages of development.

There are numerous advantages to using design patterns, as follows:

- Improves software reusability
- Development cycle becomes faster
- Makes the code more readable and maintainable
- Increases the efficiency and enhances the overall software development
- Provides common vocabulary to describe problems and best possible solutions in a more abstract way

And you can count many more. In the following sections, we will gain a deep understanding of how to make your code modular, loosely coupled, independent, testable, and maintainable, by following certain principles and patterns.

This chapter will cover in-depth ideas about the **Dependency Inversion Principle (DIP)**, the Inversion of Control paradigm, and DI design pattern.

 Most developers use the terms *design principle* and *design pattern* interchangeably, even though there is a difference between them.

Design principle: Generically, this is a guideline about what is the right way and what is the wrong way to design your application. Design principles always talk about what to do instead of how to do it.

Design patterns: A generic and reusable solution for commonly occurring problems. Design patterns talk about how to solve the problems in a given software design context by providing clear methodologies.

The first step towards making your code cleaner, readable, decoupled, maintainable, and modular is to learn the design principle called **DIP**.

Dependency Inversion Principle

DIP provides high-level guidance to make your code loosely coupled. It says the following:

- High-level modules should not depend on low-level modules for their responsibilities. Both should depend on abstractions.
- Abstractions should not depend on details. Details should depend on abstractions.

Changes are always risky when they're made in dependent code. DIP talks about keeping a chunk of code (dependency) away from the main program to which it is not directly related.

To reduce the coupling, DIP suggests eliminating the direct dependency of low-level modules on high-level modules to perform their responsibilities. Instead, make the high-level module rely on abstraction (a contract) that forms the generic low-level behavior.

This way, the actual implementation of low-level modules can be changed without making any changes in high-level modules. This produces great flexibility and molecularity in the system. As far as any low-level implementation is bound to abstraction, high-level modules can invoke it.

Let's have a look at a sample suboptimal design where we can apply DIP to improve the structure of the application.

Consider a scenario where you are designing a module that simply generates balance sheets for a local store. You are fetching data from a database, processing it with complex business logic, and exporting it into HTML format. If you design this in a procedural way, then the flow of the system would be something like the following diagram:

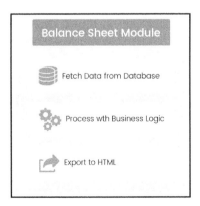

A single module takes care of fetching data, applying business logic to generate balance sheet data, and exporting it into HTML format. This is not the best design. Let's separate the whole functionality into three different modules, as shown in the following diagram:

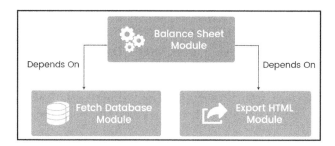

- **Fetch Database Module :** This will fetch data from a database
- **Export HTML Module:** This will export the data in HTML
- **Balance Sheet Module:** This will take data from a database module, process it, and give it to the export module to export it in HTML

In this case, the balance sheet module is a high-level module, and fetch database and export HTML are low-level modules.

The code of the `FetchDatabase` module should look something like the following snippet:

```
public class FetchDatabase {
    public List<Object[]> fetchDataFromDatabase(){
        List<Object[]> dataFromDB = new ArrayList<Object[]>();
        //Logic to call database, execute a query and fetch the data
        return dataFromDB;
    }
}
```

The `ExportHTML` module will take the list of data and export it into HTML file format. The code should look as follows:

```
public class ExportHTML {
    public File exportToHTML(List<Object[]> dataLst){
        File outputHTML = null;
        //Logic to iterate the dataLst and generate HTML file.
        return outputHTML;
    }
}
```

The code for our parent module—the `BalanceSheet` module that takes the data from the fetch database module and sends to the export HTML module—should look as follows:

```
public class BalanceSheet {
    private ExportHTML exportHTML = new ExportHTML();
    private FetchDatabase fetchDatabase = new FetchDatabase();
    public void generateBalanceSheet(){
      List<Object[]> dataFromDB =
      fetchDatabase.fetchDataFromDatabase();
        exportHTML.exportToHTML(dataFromDB);
    }
}
```

At first glance, this design looks good, as we separated the responsibilities of fetching and exporting the data into individual child modules. Good design can accommodate any future changes without breaking the system. Will this design make our system fragile in case of any future changes? Let us have a look at that.

After some time, you need to fetch the data from external web services along with the database. Also, you need to export the data in PDF format rather than HTML format. To incorporate this change, you will create new classes/modules to fetch data from web services and to export the PDF as per the following snippet:

```
// Separate child module for fetch the data from web service.
public class FetchWebService {
    public List<Object[]> fetchDataFromWebService(){
        List<Object[]> dataFromWebService = new ArrayList<Object[]>();
        //Logic to call Web Service and fetch the data and return it.
        return dataFromWebService;
    }
}
// Separate child module for export in PDF
public class ExportPDF {
    public File exportToPDF(List<Object[]> dataLst){
        File pdfFile = null;
        //Logic to iterate the dataLst and generate PDF file
        return pdfFile;
    }
}
```

To accommodate the new ways of fetching and exporting data, the balance sheet module needs some sort of flag. Based on the value of this flag, the respective child module will be instantiated in the balance sheet module. The updated code of the `BalanceSheet` module would be as follows:

```
public class BalanceSheet {

    private ExportHTML exportHTML = null;
    private FetchDatabase fetchDatabase = null;
    private ExportPDF exportPDF = null;
    private FetchWebService fetchWebService = null;

    public void generateBalanceSheet(int inputMethod, int outputMethod){
        //1. Instantiate the low level module object.
        if(inputMethod == 1){
            fetchDatabase = new FetchDatabase();
        }else if(inputMethod == 2){
            fetchWebService = new FetchWebService();
        }
        //2. fetch and export the data for specific format based on flags.
        if(outputMethod == 1){
            List<Object[]> dataLst = null;
            if(inputMethod == 1){
                dataLst = fetchDatabase.fetchDataFromDatabase();
            }else{
                dataLst = fetchWebService.fetchDataFromWebService();
            }
            exportHTML.exportToHTML(dataLst);
        }else if(outputMethod ==2){
            List<Object[]> dataLst = null;
            if(inputMethod == 1){
                dataLst = fetchDatabase.fetchDataFromDatabase();
            }else{
                dataLst = fetchWebService.fetchDataFromWebService();
            }
            exportPDF.exportToPDF(dataLst);
        }
    }
}
```

Great work! Our application is able to handle two different input and output methods to generate balance sheets. But wait a minute; what happens when you need to add more methods (fetch and export data) in the future? For example, you might need to fetch the data from google drive and export the balance sheet in Excel format.

For every new method of input and output, you need to update your main module, the balance sheet module. When a module is dependent on another concrete implementation, it's said to be tightly coupled on that. This breaks the fundamental principle: open for extension but closed for modification.

Let's recall what DIP talks about: high-level modules should not depend on low-level modules for their responsibilities. Both should depend on abstractions.

This is the fundamental problem in our design. In our case, the balance sheet (high-level) module tightly depends on fetch database and export HTML data (low-level) modules.

As we have seen, principles always show the solution to design problems. It doesn't talk about how to implement it. In our case, DIP talks about removing the tight dependency of low-level modules on high-level modules.

But how do we do that? This is where IoC comes into the picture. IoC shows a way of defining abstraction between modules. In short, IoC is the way to implement DIP.

Inversion of Control

IoC is a design methodology used to build a loosely coupled system in software engineering by inverting the control of flow from your main program to some other entity or framework.

Here, the control refers to any additional activities a program is handling other than its main activities, such as creating and maintaining the dependency objects, managing the application flow, and so on.

Unlike procedural programming style, where a program handles multiple unrelated things all together, IoC defines a guideline where you need to break the main program in multiple independent programs (modules) based on responsibility and arrange them in such a way that they are loosely coupled.

In our example, we break the functionality into separate modules. The missing part was how to arrange them to make them decoupled, and we will learn how IoC makes that arrangement. By inverting (changing) the control, your application becomes decoupled, testable, extensible, and maintainable.

Implementing DIP through IoC

DIP suggests that high-level modules should not depend on low-level modules. Both should depend on abstraction. IoC provides a way to achieve the abstraction between high-level and low-level modules.

Let's see how we can apply DIP through IoC on our Balance Sheet example. The fundamental design problem is that high-level modules (balance sheet) tightly depend on low-level (fetch and export data) modules.

Our goal is to break this dependency. To achieve this, IoC suggests inverting the control. In IoC, inverting the control can be achieved in the following ways:

- **Inverting the interface**: Make sure the high-level module defines the interface, and low-level modules follow it
- **Inverting object creation**: Change the creation of dependency from your main modules to some other program or framework
- **Inverting flow**: Change the flow of application

Inverting the interface

Inverting the interface means inverting the interaction control from low-level modules to high-level modules. Your high-level module should decide which low-level modules can interact with it, rather than keep changing itself to integrate each new low-level module.

After inverting the interface, our design would be as per the following diagram:

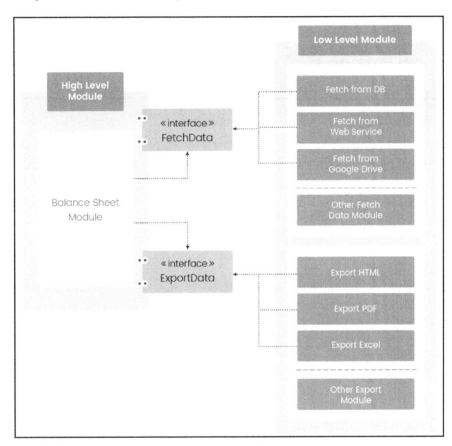

In this design, the balance sheet module (high-level) is interacting with fetch data and export data (low-level) modules with common interface. The very clear benefits of this design are that you can add new fetch data and export data (low-level) modules without changing anything on the balance sheet module (high-level).

As far as low-level modules are compatible with the interface, the high-level modules will be happy to work with it. With this new design, high-level modules are not dependent on low-level modules, and both are interacting through an abstraction (interface). Separating the interface from the implementation is a prerequisite to achieve DIP.

Let's change our code as per this new design. First, we need to create two interfaces: to fetch the data and export the data as follows:

```
public interface IFetchData {
    //Common interface method to fetch data.
    List<Object[]> fetchData();
}
public interface IExportData {
    //Common interface method to export data.
    File exportData(List<Object[]> listData);
}
```

Next, all low-level modules must implement these interfaces as per the following snippet:

```
public class FetchDatabase implements IFetchData {
    public List<Object[]> fetchData(){
        List<Object[]> dataFromDB = new ArrayList<Object[]>();
        //Logic to call database, execute a query and fetch the data
        return dataFromDB;
    }
}

public class FetchWebService implements IFetchData {
    public List<Object[]> fetchData(){
        List<Object[]> dataFromWebService = new ArrayList<Object[]>();
        //Logic to call Web Service and fetch the data and return it.
        return dataFromWebService;
    }
}

public class ExportHTML implements IExportData{
    public File exportData(List<Object[]> listData){
        File outputHTML = null;
        //Logic to iterate the listData and generate HTML File
        return outputHTML;
    }
}
public class ExportPDF implements IExportData{
    public File exportData(List<Object[]> dataLst){
        File pdfFile = null;
        //Logic to iterate the listData and generate PDF file
        return pdfFile;
    }

}
```

Finally, the balance sheet module needs to rely on interfaces to interact with low-level modules. So the updated `BalanceSheet` module should look like the following snippet:

```
public class BalanceSheet {
   private IExportData exportDataObj= null;
   private IFetchData fetchDataObj= null;

   public Object generateBalanceSheet(){
      List<Object[]> dataLst = fetchDataObj.fetchData();
      return exportDataObj.exportData(dataLst);
   }
}
```

You may have observed that, the `generateBalanceSheet()` method became more straightforward. It allows us to work with additional fetch and export modules without any change. It is thanks to the mechanism of inverting the interface that makes this possible.

This design looks perfect; but still, there is one problem. If you noticed, the balance sheet module is still keeping the responsibility of creating low-level module objects (`exportDataObj` and `fetchDataObj`). In other words, object creation dependency is still with the high-level modules.

Because of this, the Balance Sheet module is not 100 percent decoupled from the low-level modules, even after implementing interface inversion. You will end up instantiating low-level modules with if/else blocks based on some flag, and the high-level module keeps changing for adding additional low-level modules integration.

To overcome this, you need to invert the object creation from your higher-level module to some other entity or framework. This is the second way of implementing IoC.

Inverting object creation

Once the abstraction between modules is set, there is no need to keep the logic of creating dependency objects in higher-level modules. Let us understand the importance of inversion of object creation design with one more example.

Suppose you are designing a war game. Your player can shoot the enemy with various weapons. You created separate classes (low-level module) for each of the weapons. While playing the game, your player can add the weapon based on points earned.

Also, the player can change the weapon. To implement inversion of interface, we created an interface called Weapon, which will be implemented by all weapon modules, as per the following diagram:

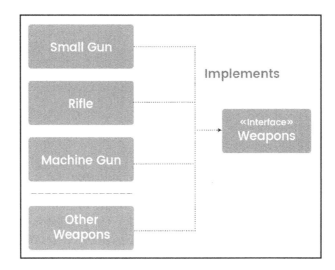

Assume that there are three weapons initially that you kept in the game. If you keep weapon creation code in your player module, the logic of choosing a weapon would be as per the following snippet:

```
public class Player {
  private Weapon weaponInHand;
  public void chooseWeapon(int weaponFlag){
    if(weaponFlag == 1){
      weaponInHand = new SmallGun();
    }else if(weaponFlag ==2){
      weaponInHand = new Rifle();
    }else{
      weaponInHand = new MachineGun();
    }
  }
  public void fireWeapon(){
    if(this.weaponInHand !=null){
      this.weaponInHand.fire();
    }
  }
}
```

Since the player module is taking care of creating the object of weapons, we are passing a flag in the `chooseWeapon()` method. Let us assume that, over a period of time, you add a few more weapons to the game. You end up changing the code of the `Player` module every time you add a new weapon.

The solution to this problem is to invert the object creation process from your main module to another entity or framework.

Let's first apply this solution to our `Player` module. The updated code would be as follows:

```
public class Player {
  private Weapon weaponInHand;
  public void chooseWeapon(Weapon setWeapon){
    this.weaponInHand = setWeapon;
  }
  public void fireWeapon(){
    if(this.weaponInHand !=null){
      this.weaponInHand.fire();
    }
  }
}
```

You can observe the following things:

- In the `chooseWeapon()` method, we are passing the object of weapons through the interface. The `Player` module is no longer handling the creation of weapon objects.
- This way, the `Player` (higher-level) module is completely decoupled from `Weapon` (low-level) modules.
- Both modules interact through the interface, defined by higher-level modules.
- For any new weapon added into the system, you do not need to change anything in the player module.

Let's apply this solution (invert creating object) to our balance sheet module. The updated code for the `BalanceSheet` module would be as per the following snippet:

```
public class BalanceSheet {

  private IExportData exportDataObj= null;
  private IFetchData fetchDataObj= null;
  //Set the fetch data object from outside of this class.
  public void configureFetchData(IFetchData actualFetchDataObj){
    this.fetchDataObj = actualFetchDataObj;
  }
  //Set the export data object from outside of this class.
```

```
public void configureExportData(IExportData actualExportDataObj){
  this.exportDataObj = actualExportDataObj;
}
public Object generateBalanceSheet(){
  List<Object[]> dataLst = fetchDataObj.fetchData();
  return exportDataObj.exportData(dataLst);
}
}
```

Here are some quick observations:

- Objects of fetch data and export data modules are created outside the balance sheet module, and passed through `configureFetchData()` and `configureExportData()` methods
- The balance sheet module is now 100 percent decoupled from fetch data and export data modules
- For any new type of fetch and export data, no change is required in balance sheet modules

At this moment, the relation between DIP and IoC can be described as per the following diagram:

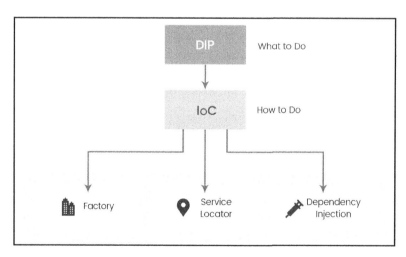

Finally, we implemented **DIP** through **IoC** and solved one of the most fundamental problems of interdependency between modules.

But hold on, something is not complete yet. We have seen that keeping the object creation away from your main module will eliminate the risk of accommodating changes and make your code decoupled. But we haven't explored how to create and pass the dependency object from outside code into your module. There are various ways of inverting object creation.

Different ways to invert object creation

We have seen how inversion of object creation helps us to decouple the modules. You can achieve the inversion of object creation with multiple design patterns as follows:

- Factory pattern
- Service locator
- Dependency injection

Inversion of object creation through the factory pattern

The factory pattern takes the responsibility of creating an object from a client who uses it. It generates the object of classes that are following a common interface. A client has to pass only type of the implementation it wants and the factory will create that object.

If we apply the factory pattern to our balance sheet example, the process of inverting of object creation is depicted as per the following diagram:

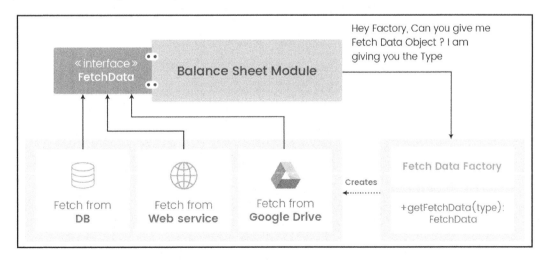

- Client (in our case, it's a balance sheet module) talks to the factory—Hey factory, can you please give me the fetch data object? Here is the type.
- The factory takes the type, creates the object, and passes it to the client (the balance sheet module).
- The factory can create the object of the same type only.
- The factory class is a complete black box for its clients. They know it's a static method to get objects.

The Balance Sheet module can get `FetchData` objects from `FetchDataFactory`. The code of `FetchDataFactory` will be as follows:

```
public class FetchDataFactory {
  public static IFetchData getFetchData(String type){
    IFetchData fetchData = null;
    if("FROM_DB".equalsIgnoreCase(type)){
      fetchData = new FetchDatabase();
    }else if("FROM_WS".equalsIgnoreCase(type)){
      fetchData = new FetchWebService();
    }else {
      return null;
    }
    return fetchData;
  }
}
```

To use this factory, you need to update the `configureFetchData()` method of a balance sheet module as follows:

```
//Set the fetch data object from Factory.
  public void configureFetchData(String type){
    this.fetchDataObj = FetchDataFactory.getFetchData(type);
  }
```

For export data, you need to create a separate factory as per the following snippet:

```
public class ExportDataFactory {

  public static IExportData getExportData(String type){
    IExportData exportData = null;
    if("TO_HTML".equalsIgnoreCase(type)){
      exportData = new ExportHTML();
    }else if("TO_PDF".equalsIgnoreCase(type)){
      exportData = new ExportPDF();
    }else {
      return null;
    }
```

```
        return exportData;
    }
}
```

If a new fetch data or export data type is introduced, you need to change it in its respective factory class only.

Inversion of object creation through service locator

The service locator pattern works more or less the same as to the factory pattern. The service locator can find the existing object and send it to the client rather than create a new one every time, as with the factory pattern. Instead of getting into detail, we will just look briefly at how the service locator works to create objects. The flow of the service locator can be described as per the following diagram:

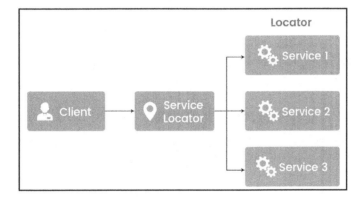

- **Client** is relying on **Service Locator** to find services. Here, *service* means any kind of dependency
- **Service Locator** takes the name of the service, and returns the object of service back to the client

If our balance sheet module uses the service locator, the code of the `configureFetchData()` method would be like the following snippet:

```
//Set the fetch data object from ServiceLocator.
  public void configureFetchData(String type){
     this.fetchDataObj =
FetchDataServiceLocator.Instance.getFetchData(type);
  }
```

Similar to fetch data, you need to design a separate service locator for export data. For any new fetch data or export data type, the changes need to be done in the service locator.

Another way of inverting the object creation is DI.

Dependency injection

DI is one of the ways to invert the object creation process from your module to other code or entity. The term *injection* refers to the process of passing the dependent object into a software component.

Since DI is one of the ways to implement **IoC**, it relies on abstraction to set the dependency. The client object doesn't know which class will be used to provide functionality at compile time. The dependency will be resolved at runtime.

A dependent object does not directly call to the client object; instead, the client object will call a dependent object whenever required. It's similar to the Hollywood principle: Don't call us, we'll call you when we need to.

Dependency injection types

In DI, you need to set the entry point in a client object from which the dependency can be injected. Based on these entry points, DI can be implemented with the following types:

- Constructor injection
- Setter injection
- Interface injection

Constructor injection

This is the most common way to inject dependency. In this approach, you need to pass the dependent object through a public constructor of a client object. Please note that in case of construction injection, you need to pass all the dependency objects in the constructor of a client object.

Constructor injection can control the order of instantiation and consequently reduce the risk of circular dependency. All mandatory dependencies can be passed through constructor injection.

In our `BalanceSheet` example, we need to pass two objects in a constructor, because it has two dependencies: one is for fetch data, and the second is for export data types, as per the following snippet:

```
public class BalanceSheet {

  private IExportData exportDataObj= null;
  private IFetchData fetchDataObj= null;
  //All dependencies are injected from client's constructor
  BalanceSheet(IFetchData fetchData, IExportData exportData){
    this.fetchDataObj = fetchData;
    this.exportDataObj = exportData;
  }
  public Object generateBalanceSheet(){
    List<Object[]> dataLst = fetchDataObj.fetchData();
    return exportDataObj.exportData(dataLst);
  }
}
```

All dependencies are injected from a constructor of a client object. Since constructors are called only once, it's clear that the dependency object will not be changed until the existence of a client object. If a client uses constructor injection, then extending and overriding it would be difficult sometimes.

Setter injection

As its name suggests, here dependency injection is done through setter methods exposed publicly. Any dependency not required at the time of client object instantiation is called **optional dependency**. They can be set at a later stage after a client object is created.

Setter injection is a perfect fit for optional or conditional dependency. Let's apply a setter injection to the `BalanceSheet` module.

The code would look as follows:

```
public class BalanceSheet {

  private IExportData exportDataObj= null;
  private IFetchData fetchDataObj= null;
  //Setter injection for Export Data
  public void setExportDataObj(IExportData exportDataObj) {
    this.exportDataObj = exportDataObj;
  }

  //Setter injection for Fetch Data
```

```
  public void setFetchDataObj(IFetchData fetchDataObj) {
    this.fetchDataObj = fetchDataObj;
  }

  public Object generateBalanceSheet(){
    List<Object[]> dataLst = fetchDataObj.fetchData();
    return exportDataObj.exportData(dataLst);
  }
}
```

For each dependency, you need to put separate setter methods. Since the dependencies are set through the setter method, the object or a framework which supplies the dependencies need to call the setter methods at an appropriate time to make sure dependencies are available before a client object starts using it.

Interface injection

Interface injection defines a way by which the dependency provider should talk to a client. It abstracts the process of passing dependency. The dependency provider defines an interface that all clients need to implement. This method is not so frequently used.

Technically, interface injection and setter injection are the same. They both use some sort of method to inject dependency. However, for interface injection, the method is defined by objects which provide the dependency.

Let's apply interface injection to our balance sheet module:

```
public interface IFetchAndExport {
  void setFetchData(IFetchData fetchData);
  void setExportData(IExportData exportData);
}

//Client class implements interface
public class BalanceSheet implements IFetchAndExport {

  private IExportData exportDataObj= null;
  private IFetchData fetchDataObj= null;
  //Implements the method of interface injection to set dependency
  @Override
  public void setFetchData(IFetchData fetchData) {
    this.fetchDataObj = fetchData;
  }

  //Implements the method of interface injection to set dependency
  @Override
```

```
public void setExportData(IExportData exportData) {
  this.exportDataObj = exportData;
}

public Object generateBalanceSheet(){
  List<Object[]> dataLst = fetchDataObj.fetchData();
  return exportDataObj.exportData(dataLst);
}
}
```

We have created interface IFetchAndExport and defined methods to inject dependencies. The dependency provider class knows how to pass the dependency through this interface. Our client object (Balance Sheet module) implements this method to set dependencies.

IoC containers

So far, we have talked about the code or framework that plays the role of dependency provider. It can be any custom code or full-fledged **IoC** container. Some developers refer to it as a *DI container*, but we will simply call it a *container*.

If we write custom code to supply dependency, things get smoother until we have just a single level of dependency. Take the scenario where our client classes are also dependent of some other modules. This results in chained or nested dependencies.

In this situation, implementing dependency injection will become quite complicated through manual code. That is where we need to rely on containers.

A container takes care of creating, configuring, and managing objects. You just need to do configuration, and the container will take care of object instantiation and dependency management with ease. You don't need to write any custom code such as that we wrote while implementing **IoC** with factory or service locator patterns.

So, as a developer, your life is cool. You just give a hint about your dependency, and the container will handle the rest and you can focus on implementing business logic.

If we choose containers to set dependencies for our Balance Sheet module, the container will create the objects of all dependencies first. Then, it will create an object of the Balance Sheet class and pass the dependencies in it. A container will do all these things silently and give you the object of the Balance Sheet module with all dependencies set in it. This process can be described with the following diagram:

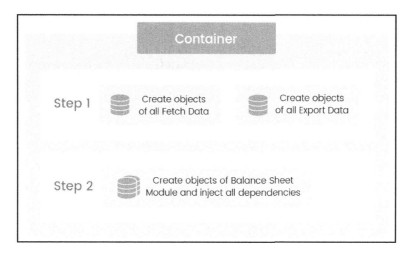

In conclusion, the following are the advantages of using containers over manual code to manage dependency:

- Isolating the process of object creation from your code and making your code more clean and readable.
- Removing object wiring (setting dependency) code from your client module. The container will take care of object wiring.
- Making your modules 100 percent loose coupling.
- Managing the entire lifecycle of the modules. This is very helpful when you want to configure the objects for various scopes, such as request, session, and so on in application execution.
- Swapping out the dependency is just a matter of configuration—no change is required in the code.
- It is a more centralized way to handle object life span and dependency management. This is useful when you want to apply some common logic across the dependencies, for example, AOP in Spring. We will see details about AOP in Chapter 6, *Aspect-Oriented Programming and Interceptors*.
- Your module can benefit from advanced features that ship with containers.

Spring, Google Guice, and Dagger are some of the IoC containers available today for Java. Starting from Enterprise Edition version 6, Java introduced **Context Dependency Injection (CDI)**, a dependency injection framework in Enterprise Edition. It's more or less similar to Spring's annotation-based DI implementation. Out of all the preceding containers, Spring is the most popular and widely used IoC container today.

Summary

In the software paradigm, it's always recommended to break the whole system down into small modules that can work independently for specific tasks. DIP is one of the important principles to build a modular system. In this chapter, we saw how high-level modules should not depend on low-level modules, and both should depend on abstraction (the concept of DIP).

We learned in detail how we can achieve DIP through IoC. Setting inversion of control makes a system loosely coupled. We also learned various design patterns such as factory, service locator, and dependency injection to implement IoC.

After that, we learned about the various types of the dependency injection pattern. Finally, we discussed **IoC** containers and how they're useful when building modular systems.

In the next chapter, we will talk about modularity concepts and dependency injection in Java 9.

Dependency Injection in Java 9 2

In the previous chapter, we got acquainted with the Dependency Injection Principle, IOC with different scenarios, and different types of Dependency Injection by writing code.

In this chapter, we will learn about the new features offered in Java 9. Specifically, we will learn about modularity in Java 9, modularity framework, types of modules offered in Java 9, and we will see Dependency Injection using modules.
This chapter will mainly cover the following topics:

- Java 9 introduction
- Modular Framework in Java 9
- Dependency Injection using Java 9 Modular Framework

Java 9 introduction

Before learning what's new in Java 9, we need to know one of the important components of Java, which is **Java Development Kit (JDK)**.

JDK is a collection of **Java Standard Edition (Java SE)**, **Java Enterprise Edition (Java EE)**, **Java Micro Edition** platforms **(Java ME)**, and different tools such as javac, Java console, JAR, JShell, Jlink, and it provides all the libraries for developing, debugging, and monitoring for building Java-based applications.

Java 9 has come up with almost over 100 new features and enhancements in different categories of JDK, such as tools, security, deployment, performance tuning, API changes of core libraries, and javadoc.

Key features

Let's look at some of the key features of Java 9 in brief, which will change Java software development:

- **Java Platform Module System (JPMS)**
- JShell (REPL)—The Java Shell
- JLink—Module Linker
- Multi-Release JAR Files
- Stream API enhancements
- Stack—Walking API
- Immutable collections with convenient factory methods
- Support of HTTP 2.0

Java Platform Module System

The introduction of **Java Platform Module System (JPMS)** is key and a game changer feature of Java 9 and JPMS developed under the shed of project Jigsaw.

The main objectives of project Jigsaw are as follows:

- Scalable JDK: Until Java 8, engineering of JDK is solid and contains a number of components, which make it troublesome to maintain and develop. JDK 9 is partitioned into sets of independent modules, which permits custom runtime capability to incorporate only required modules in our application, which offers assistance to diminish runtime size.
- Robust encapsulation and security: Bundles from the module can be expressly exposed if required by other modules. On the other hand, another module has to explicitly define which particular bundles are required from modules. This way, modules can encapsulate particular bundles for security purposes.
- Dependency: Modern module frameworks permit us to define unequivocal dependency between modules and all required subset modules dependency can be distinguished at compile time.
- Modern rebuild permits us to incorporate runtime images of modules, which gives superior performance of JDK. It moreover evacuates `tools.jar` and `rt.jar` from runtime images.
- To secure the internal structure of runtime images, an unused URI conspire is utilized for naming modules, resources, and classes.

We will discuss JPMS in detail in the *Modular Framework in Java 9* section.

JShell (REPL) – The Java Shell

In earlier JDK, we did not have the luxury of running code using a command line interface. For learning new functions such as the matches function of regular expression API and many more, we had to write a necessary skeleton of Java, `public static void main(String[] args)`, and go through the compilation and execution phase.

Java 9 introduced JShell, a command line tool. It uses the **Read-Eval-Print Loop** (REPL) principle to provide a command line interface to interact with the Java platform and provide an interactive way of running a program without writing necessary skeletons.

JShell came up with a parser that parses submitted code and identifies different types such as a variable, a declared method, loop, and many more, and put them all together in a dummy skeleton to make a complete Java program to pass it to the compiler. Based on the inputs compiler, it converts it into byte code. During this process, a file is not created, so it will all be saved in memory. At the end, the generated byte code is used by JVM to load and execute.

JShell is located in the `bin` directory of shipped JDK 9. Using a command interface, traverse to the `bin` directory and type command `JShell` to start the tool:

Let's consider a program that we used to write in IDE. Here is a simple program to print a string message into uppercase:

```
module javaIntroduction {
}
package com.packt.java9dependency.examples;
public class Main {
    public static void main(String[] args) {
      String s = "hello java module system".toUpperCase();
        System.out.println(s);
    }
}
```

Now, we can get quick output of the preceding string message by directly writing a statement in the JShell tool, declaring variables and `println` statements is not required. JShell provides various command features that make a developer's life easy when writing quick code snippets.

```
C:\Windows\System32\cmd.exe - jshell

C:\Program Files\Java\jdk-9.0.1\bin>jshell
|  Welcome to JShell -- Version 9.0.1
|  For an introduction type: /help intro

jshell> "hello java module system".toUpperCase();
$1 ==> "HELLO JAVA MODULE SYSTEM"

jshell>
```

JLink – Module Linker

When we are talking about modular systems, then immediately one question comes, how dependencies of modules will organize and what will be impact on final deployment?

The JLink tool is designed to provide optional phases between compile time and runtime, called link time, which links a set of modules and its transitive dependencies to create runtime images. JLink makes deployment simpler and also reduces the size of an application.

The invocation syntax of `jLink` is as follows:

```
jlink --module-path <modulepath> --add-modules <modules> --limit-modules
<modules> --output <path>

--module-path - jLink use module path for finding modules such as modular
jars, JMOD files
--add-modules - Mention module which needs to include in default set of
modules for run time image, by default set of modules in empty.
--limit-modules - Use this option to limits modules, which is required for
our application.
--output - Final resulting run time image will be stored in output
directory
--help - list details about jLink options
--version - show the version number
```

Multi-release JAR files

We have seen many third-party libraries, support for several Java versions with backward compatibility. Because of this, they don't use the latest API features introduced in new releases of JDK. Since Java 8, there is no facility to define condition-based platform dependencies for using new features.

Java 9 introduced a multi-release jar concept. It allows developers to create alternative versions of each class, which are only used when running on specific Java versions.

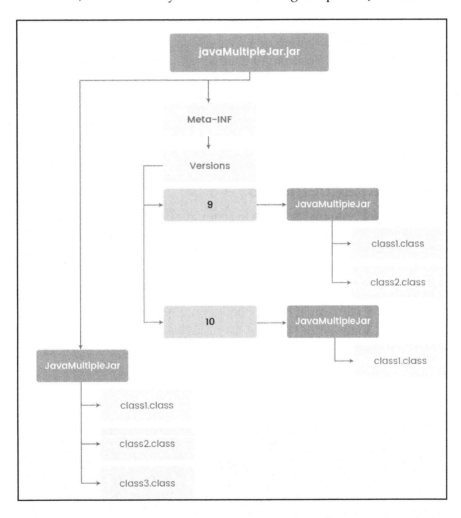

The preceding diagram shows the structure of a multi-release jar. It contain resources and classes along with the **Meta-INF** directory for metadata. This metadata file contains version-specific details to encode jar files to provide a compatible method for multiple versions of libraries that run on a target Java platform.

To continue on with the preceding example, we can see that the **javaMutipleJar** library has three classes, **Class1.class**, **Class2.class**, and **Class3.class**, at root level build with Java 8. If we deploy this jar in JDK, which does not support MARJAR, then only the root level classes will be visible and later platform classes will be ignored.

Moreover, **Class1.class** and **Class2.class** want to use Java 9 features, so then only those classes will bundle with Java 9 compilation. When Java 10 comes and **Class1.class** wants to use Java 10 features, then, as mentioned in the diagram, because of MARJAR concepts, it will bundle with the Java 10 platform.

Ultimately, multi-release jar concepts help third-party library and framework developers to easily separate the use of new APIs for specific JDK for supporting migration as well as continuing to support older versions.

Stream API enhancements

Stream is a pipeline that contains elements in sequential form to support aggregation operations on collections of data. Stream API is a major feature of Java 8, which provides sequential and parallel execution with filtering based on criteria, all this together is known as internal iteration of Stream.

Java 9 added four new methods to make the Stream API better for iterating operations. `dropWhile` and `takeWhile` methods are default methods and `iterate` and `ofNullable` are static methods in the `java.util.stream` interface. Let's discuss the `takeWhile` method use.

Stream API Syntax:

```
default Stream<T> takeWhile(Predicate<? super T> predicate)
```

```
jshell> Stream<Integer> str = Stream.of(4,5,6,7,10,8,10);
str ==> java.util.stream.ReferencePipeline$Head@7b49cea0

jshell> str.takeWhile(i -> i < 7 ).forEach(a -> System.out.println(a));
4
5
6

jshell>
```

The `takeWhile()` method returns the longest prefix, which matches the predicate for the ordered stream. As from the preceding code, `takeWhile` returns the first three elements because of matching with the predicate.

For unordered streams, the `takeWhile()` method returns a prefixed element until the predicate condition is true. It stops iteration if the predicate condition returns false and returns a list of elements that predicate evaluated until the condition fails for the first time.

Stack-walking API

To debug exceptions, we look at the root cause of exception by traversing the stack trace. Prior to Java 9, we all used `Thread.getStackTrace()` to get `StackTraceElement` objects in the form of arrays.

StackTraceElement: Each element of `StackTraceElement` is a single `StackFrame`, which provides details about classname, method name, filename, and line number where the exception was generated. Except for the first `StackFrame`, all the other elements represent the method invocation call from the starting point of the application to the point where the exception generated. This is helpful when we want auditing of generated error logs.

Java 9 StackWalker API provides several features such as filtering, asserting, and skipping certain classes in the stack trace. We can get either a full stack trace or short stack trace for a current thread at any point.

StackWalker provides various methods for capturing information about stacks, such as:

- **forEach**: For the current thread it returns each StackFrame stream to perform actions
- **getInstance()**: This returns the current instance of StackWalker
- **walk()**: This is used to open a sequential stream for each StackFrame for the current thread, where we can apply functions such as limit, skip, and filter

```
List<StackFrame> stack =
StackWalker.getInstance(StackWalker.Option.RETAIN_CLASS_REFERENCE).walk((s)
-> s.collect(Collectors.toList()));
```

The preceding snippet gives a list of all the StackFrame of the current thread by retaining class references. In the following snippet, we needed only the first 10 frames in the method and the skip frames, which are declared in the `com.packt.java9dependency` package:

```
List<StackFrame> frames = StackWalker.getInstance().walk(s -> s.dropWhile(f
->
f.getClassName().startsWith("com.packt.java9dependency")).limit(10).collect
(Collectors.toList()));
```

Immutable collections with convenient factory methods

Many times we directly add or remove elements from a collection, which is returned from the `factory` method. This collection is immutable and adding items into these collection gives us an exception called `UnSupportedOperationException`.

To avoid such situations, we create immutable collection objects by using the `collections.unmodifiableXXX()` method. These methods are also tedious, such as writing multiple statements for adding individual items and then adding into it immutable `List` or `Set` or `Map`:

```
Before Java 9,
List<String> asiaRegion = new ArrayList<String>();
asiaRegion.add("India");
asiaRegion.add("China");
asiaRegion.add("SriLanka");
List<String> unmodifiableAsiaRegionList =
Collections.unmodifiableList(asiaRegion);
```

Java 9 provides convenient immutable factory methods such as `List.of()`, `Set.of()` and `Map.of()` to solve the previously mentioned issue:

```
After Java 9,
List<String> asiaRegion = List.of("India","China","SriLanka");
Set<Integer> immutableSet = Set.of(10, 15, 20, 25);
```

HTTP/2.0 support

We used to connect servers using `HttpURLConnection`, which works in a single request/response cycle, and this eventually increases web page loading time and latency.

Moreover, the difference between HTTP/1.1 of older JDK and HTTP/2 of JAVA 9 is that data is framed when transporting between clients and servers. HTTP/2 uses the `HttpClient` API to push data by using the server push feature, with this it allows us to prioritize and send required data for loading the web page first. The following example shows HTTP interaction for the `GET` method:

```
//Get the HttpClient object
HttpClient client = HttpClient.newHttpClient();

// GET Method call
HttpResponse<String> getResponse = client.send(
    HttpRequest
        .newBuilder(new URI("http://www.xyz.com/")
        .GET()
        .build(),
    BodyHandler.asString()
);
//Response of call
int responseStatus = getResponse.statusCode();
String body = responseStatus.body();
```

Modular Framework in Java 9

In the previous section, we discussed several Java 9 features in brief. Now, in this section, we will learn about the Modular Framework and how it is used in Java 9.

What is modularity?

Before we move to Java Platform Module System, let's understand the meaning of modularity in the real world.

Modularity is a design that divides systems into smaller parts called a module. Nowadays, modular kitchens are installed in homes. These types of kitchen include several units or modules such as wall cabinets, cupboards, sinks, and many more and all these different parts are built in factories. If at any time there is damage in any unit, then only that module needs to be replaced or repaired.

Another familiar modular system is electric outlets in walls, which allow you to plug in different types of electrical gadgets such as microwaves, mixer grinders, refrigerators, televisions, and they are all designed to work on defined tasks. These devices work in any outlet without caring whether it is in our home or a neighbor's home, they just do their task and function when they are plugged in.

In terms of computer systems, modularity is a concept of combination and linking of multiple independent modules in a single system. It increases usability and removes duplication of code and also makes a system loosely coupled. Similar to the electric outlet concept, modules should do their task without caring where they are plugged into an application.

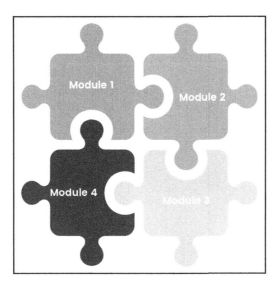

Java Platform Module System

Java Platform Module System (JPMS) is also known as JSR 376 and is implemented under project Jigsaw. We have to understand why we need module systems in Java and what the changes in current JDK are.

The need for a Java modular system

To run a small or big application, a runtime environment up to Java 8 is required because JDK is built to support monolithic design. All libraries are tightly coupled with each other and for deployment full JDK is required.

Maintainability: We all want an application to be loosely coupled, highly united, readable, and understandable. So we are using classes and packages. Day by day Java is growing exponentially in terms of size and packages to provide better features, but dependencies between packages is compromised. So we need something new that is better than packages for maintaining our code base.

JAR Hell: Before Java 9, The JVM does not have thought that how JAR on the class path depends on another Jar. It essentially loads a bunch of JARs, but it does not validate their dependencies. The JVM breaks the execution at runtime when a JAR is missing. The JARs don't characterize accessibility constraints such as open or private. The whole substance of all JARs on the class path is totally visible to all the other JARs from the class path. There is no way to declare that a few classes in a JAR are private. All classes and methods are open related to the class path. Sometimes, we have jar files that contain multiple versions of a single class. The Java ClassLoader loads only one version of this class, and it does not determined which one. This creates uncertainty about how our program is going to work. This issue is known as **JAR Hell**. The Module Path concept presented in Java 9 tends to illuminate issues caused by the class path.

Implicit Dependency: We have all seen the `NoClassDefFoundError` error a few times. It comes when JVM is not able to discover a class on which code it is executing. Finding depending code and lost dependency is simple, but dependency that is not in classLoader is troublesome to recognize, since there are chances that the same class is stacked by numerous class loaders. The current JAR framework is not able to express which other JAR file is dependent, so that JVM understands and resolves dependency.

Lack of strong encapsulation: Java's visibility modifier provides strong encapsulation between classes of the same packages. Current Java encapsulation works with ClassPath where every public class is visible to other classes because several critical JDK API classes are open for other classes.

All preceding issues are fixed with Java 9 module concepts.

Modular JDK

JDK 9 folder structure has changed compared to Java 8; JDK 9 does not have JRE, it is separately installed into a distinct folder. In JDK 9, we can see a new folder called **jmod**, which contains all the Java platform modules. Java 9 on wards `rt.jar` and `tool.jar` is not available in JDK:

Name	Date modified	Type
java.activation.jmod	11/7/2017 2:58 PM	JMOD File
java.base.jmod	11/7/2017 2:58 PM	JMOD File
java.compiler.jmod	11/7/2017 2:58 PM	JMOD File
java.corba.jmod	11/7/2017 2:58 PM	JMOD File
java.datatransfer.jmod	11/7/2017 2:58 PM	JMOD File
java.desktop.jmod	11/7/2017 2:58 PM	JMOD File
java.instrument.jmod	11/7/2017 2:58 PM	JMOD File
java.jnlp.jmod	11/7/2017 2:58 PM	JMOD File
java.logging.jmod	11/7/2017 2:58 PM	JMOD File
java.management.jmod	11/7/2017 2:58 PM	JMOD File
java.management.rmi.jmod	11/7/2017 2:58 PM	JMOD File
java.naming.jmod	11/7/2017 2:58 PM	JMOD File
java.prefs.jmod	11/7/2017 2:58 PM	JMOD File
java.rmi.jmod	11/7/2017 2:58 PM	JMOD File
java.scripting.jmod	11/7/2017 2:58 PM	JMOD File
java.se.ee.jmod	11/7/2017 2:58 PM	JMOD File
java.se.jmod	11/7/2017 2:58 PM	JMOD File
java.security.jgss.jmod	11/7/2017 2:58 PM	JMOD File
java.security.sasl.jmod	11/7/2017 2:58 PM	JMOD File
java.smartcardio.jmod	11/7/2017 2:58 PM	JMOD File
java.sql.jmod	11/7/2017 2:58 PM	JMOD File

All Java modules, `src` are available from the `..\jdk-9.0.1\lib\src` folder, and each module includes `module-info.java`. The following is a diagram that shows how JDK looks with all modules:

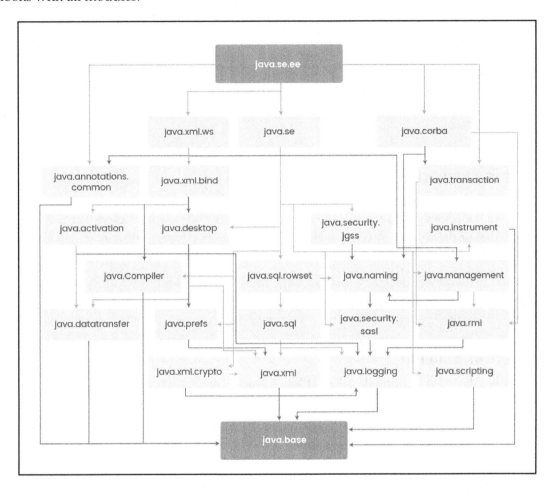

Every other module implicitly or explicitly depends on the `java.base` module. It follows a directed acyclic graph dependency, which means no circular dependency is allowed between modules.

All modules in JDK 9 are by default dependent on the base module, known as the `java.base` module. It includes the `java.lang` package.

We can list all modules of Java 9 using the command `-- list-modules`. Each module name is followed by a version number with string `-@9`, to indicate that the module belongs to Java 9. A JDK 9 specific module is prefix with keyword *jdk* such as `jdk.compiler` and JAVA SE specific modules start with the *java keyword*.

What is a module?

When we discuss modular systems, immediately you might ask what is a module? A module is a collection of code, data, and resources with self-descriptive properties. It contains a set of packages and types such as classes, abstract classes, interfaces, and so on, and also, most importantly, every module contains a `module-info.java` file.

A module can explicitly declare which package needs to export for other modules and what is required from other modules in order to compile and run. This will also help us to identify which module is missing when we get an error.

Structure of a module

Modules are the main building block of JPMS. Modules are similar to JARs, but have additional characteristics, such as:

- **Module Name**: A unique name to identify globally; a name can be defined by using inverse-URL naming convention
- Declare dependencies for other modules
- Declaration of API that needs to export as packages

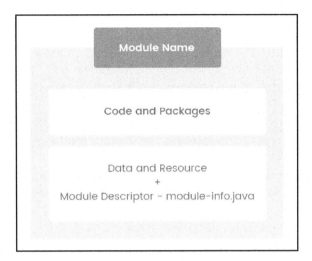

Module Descriptor (module-info.java)

`module-info.java` is an important file in the modular system, and it contains modular metadata which describes the behavior module. It is a Java file, but it is not like a traditional Java file. It has its own syntax and it's compiled into the `module-info.class` file.

The following is the syntax that we have to follow when creating `module-info.java`:

```
module <module-name> {
        requires <module-name-1>;
        requires <module-name-2>;
                .

                .
        requires <module-name-n>;
        exports <package-1>;
                .

                .
        exports <package-n>;
}
```

The following is an example of the `module-info.java` file, where each module contains a unique ID and optional module descriptor details:

```
module com.packt.java9dependency.chapter2 {
  exports com.packt.java9dependency.chapter2.services;
  requires com.packt.java9dependency.chapter1;
  requires java.sql;
}
```

Let's understand different module descriptors, mentioned here:

- **requires <module>**: This descriptor specifies that a module depends on another module to run this module, this type of relationship is called a *module dependency*. At runtime, modules only see modules that are required, and this is called Readability.
- **requires transitive <module>**: This means to indicate a dependency on another module and, moreover, to guarantee that other modules perusing your module read that dependency—known as implied readability. For example, module A reads module B and module B reads module C, then module B needs to declare requires transitive, otherwise module A will not compile unless they read module C explicitly.
- **requires static <module>**: By using a static keyword, dependency will be validated at compile time and it will be optional at runtime.
- **exports <package-name>**: This descriptor is used to export own packages to other modules.
- **exports <package-name> to <module-name>**: By using such descriptor statements, we export packages to specific modules, not to all modules. It's called qualified export.
- **opens <package-name>**: Opens descriptor used to define, only public types of packages are accessible to code in other modules at runtime only using reflection.
- **opens <package-name> to <module-name>**: A qualified open. This opens only a specific module that can access public type packages at runtime only through reflection.
- **uses <service-interface>**: A module directive defined service used for this module. It makes a module as a service consumer. Service implementation can be in the same module or on another module.
- **provide <service-interface> with <class1>,<class2>** : Specifies that a module contains service implementation of an interface defined in a modules's uses descriptor. This makes a module a service provider.

The following are important points that we need to understand when creating a module descriptor:

- A module-info can have only a module name; means exports or requires clause are not mandatory.
- If a module descriptor has only exports then it means it is only exporting declared packages to other modules and it is not dependent on any other module. We can call them independent modules. For example, the `java.base` module.

- Opposite to the previous point, module descriptors might contain export and requires clauses, which means the module is exporting packages to other modules and is also dependent on other modules for its own compilation.
- There might be zero or more export or requires clauses in the module descriptor.

 When we create a project, JDK 8 adds a JDK jar into our project ClassPath. But when we create a Java 9 module project, then JDK modules are added into ModulePath.

Module types

There are different types of modules:

Named application modules: This is a simple module that we can all create. Any third-party libraries can be application modules.

Platform modules: As we have seen, JDK 9 itself migrated to modular architecture. All the existing features will be provided as different modules, such as `java.sql`, `java.desktop`, `java.transaction`. These are called Platform Modules. All modules are implicitly dependent on the `java.base` module.

Automatic modules: A pre-Java 9 JAR, which is not migrated to modules, can be placed in a module path without module descriptors. These are called automated modules. This JAR implicitly exports all their packages for other modules and also reads other modules along with unnamed modules. Because there is no unique name for an automatic module, JDK generates depending on the JAR filename by removing the version number and extension. For example, the file `postgresql-42.1.4.jar` as a module will be `postgresql`.

Unnamed modules: JDK 9 does not remove classpaths. So all the JARs and classes placed on the class path are called Unnamed Modules. These modules can read all the modules and export all the packages, as they do not have a name. This module cannot be read or required by named application modules.

In JDK 9, we have two module paths and class paths. Now we might ask which JAR goes where? So, the answer is, a modular jar with an application module goes into `--module-path`, and a modular jar with an unnamed module can be placed into `--class-path`. Similarly, a non-modular jar can be migrated into an automatic module and goes into `--module-path`. If a jar contains an unnamed module, then it resides in `--class-path`.

Dependency Injection using the Java 9 Modular Framework

The last topic we will learn about is molecularity and basics of Java 9 modules. Now, we will learn how to write modules and how Dependency Injection is handled in modules.

Java 9 has the concept of Service Loader, which is related to IoC and Dependency Injection. New module systems do not provide Dependency Injection, but the same can be achieved by Service Loader and SPI (Service Provider Interface) Pattern. We will now see how this will work with Java 9.

Modules with Service Loader

A service is a bunch of interfaces and classes collectively named a library, which delivers a specific functionality. Simply, we can say API. There are multiple usages for a service and they are called service providers (say implementations) . The client utilizing this service will not have any contact with the implementations. This can be accomplished by utilizing the underneath concept.

Java has `ClassLoader`, which simply loads the classes and creates instances of classes on runtime. Compared to Java 9 modules, `java.util.ServiceLoader` is capable of finding and loading all the service providers at a runtime for a service interface. The `ServiceLoader` class permits decoupling between the API and client app. The service loader will instantiate all the service providers that are implementing the service and makes it accessible to the client to utilize.

Let's take an example of Notification Application containing API and a different implementation of API. We will create three modules, the first one with a service (API) module, the second one will be a provider (Implementation) module, and the last one will be a client module for the accessing service.

Service (API) module

The created API module with the name `com.packt.service.api` contains a `NotificationService` interface to send notification and load service providers. To make this interface a service provider interface (SPI), we have to mention the `'use'` clause in `module-info.java`. Our module code will be as follows:

```
NotificationService.java

package com.packt.service.api;

import java.util.ArrayList;
import java.util.List;
import java.util.ServiceLoader;

public interface NotificationService {
  /* Loads all the service providers */
  public static List<NotificationService> getInstances() {
    ServiceLoader<NotificationService> services =
ServiceLoader.load(NotificationService.class);
    List<NotificationService> list = new ArrayList<>();
    services.iterator().forEachRemaining(list::add);
    return list;
  }
  /* Send notification with provided message and recipient */
  boolean sendNotification(String message, String recipient);
}
```

`module-info.java` will be as follows:

```
module com.packt.service.api {
  exports com.packt.service.api;
  uses com.packt.service.api.NotificationService;
}
```

The following are the command line steps that need to be followed for the `com.packt.service.api` module jar. Assume that there will be an out directory in the `com.packt.service.api` module:

```
D:\java9di\java9-di-service-loader\com.packt.service.api>javac -d out src/module-info.java src/com/packt/service/api/NotificationService.java
D:\java9di\java9-di-service-loader\com.packt.service.api>jar --create --file notification-api.jar -C out .
```

Service provider (Implementation) module

Now, create a service provider module `com.packt.service.impl` to implement `NotificationService` service API, and for that we should define a *"provides ... with"* clause in the `module-info.java` file. The ***provides*** keyword is used to mention the service interface name and the ***with*** keyword is used to mention which implementation we want to load. In the event that the module doesn't have the provides statement in the module descriptor file, the service loader will not load that module. The syntax of the *'provides...with'* statement is as follows:

```
provides <service-interface> with <service-implementation>
```

To send an SMS message to a recipient we are creating two implementation classes, `SMSServiceImpl.java` and `EmailServiceImpl`, by implementing `NotificationService`:

```
SMSServiceImpl.java

package com.packt.service.impl;

import com.packt.service.api.NotificationService;

public class SMSServiceImpl implements NotificationService {

  public boolean sendNotification(String message, String recipient) {
    // Code to send SMS
    System.out.println("SMS has been sent to Recipient :: " + recipient + "
with Message :: "+message);
    return true;
  }
}
```

The module descriptor for this provider module will be as follows:

```
module-info.java

module com.packt.service.impl {
  requires com.packt.service.api;
  provides com.packt.service.api.NotificationService with
com.packt.service.impl.SMSServiceImpl;

}
```

To generate a jar file of the `com.packt.service.impl` module, we have to copy `notification-api.jar` of the service API module into the lib folder for compile time dependency resolution. The outcome of the following commands will be `sms-service.jar`:

```
D:\java9di\java9-di-service-loader\com.packt.service.impl>mkdir lib

D:\java9di\java9-di-service-loader\com.packt.service.impl>copy ..\com.packt.service.api\notification-api.jar lib\notification-api.jar
        1 file(s) copied.

D:\java9di\java9-di-service-loader\com.packt.service.impl>javac -d out --module-path lib src/module-info.java src/com/packt/service/impl/SMSServiceImpl.java

D:\java9di\java9-di-service-loader\com.packt.service.impl>jar --create --file sms-service.jar -C out .
```

Service Provider Rules:

- It always has a no-argument constructor. This constructor is used by the `ServiceLoader` class to instantiate the service provider using reflection.
- The provider must be a public concrete class. It should not be an abstract class or inner class.
- An occurrence of the implementation class must be consistent with the service interface.

Service client application

Now, create a client application named `com.packt.client`, which lists all implementation of `NotificationService` by calling the `getInstances()` method. A client application only *requires* the `com.packt.service.api` module as dependency in `module-info.java`. But we have to copy `notification-api.jar` and `sms-service.jar` into the lib folder to resolve compile time dependency of the service API and service provider module. Our `ClientApplication.java` and `module-info.java` will look as follows:

```
ClientApplication.java

package com.packt.client;

import java.util.List;
import com.packt.service.api.NotificationService;

public class ClientApplication {

   public static void main(String[] args) {
      List<NotificationService> notificationServices =
NotificationService.getInstances();
         for (NotificationService services : notificationServices) {
```

```
            services.sendNotification("Hello", "1234567890");
        }
    }
}
```

For our client application, we have to only mention the *requires* clause for
com.packt.service.api in the module-info.java file:

```
module-info.java

module com.packt.client {
    requires com.packt.service.api;
}
```

The following are commands that need to run in order to run our client application. In the
output we will get a message from SMSServiceImpl.java:

```
D:\java9di\java9-di-service-loader\com.packt.client>mkdir lib

D:\java9di\java9-di-service-loader\com.packt.client>copy ..\com.packt.service.api\notification-api.jar lib\notification-api.jar
        1 file(s) copied.

D:\java9di\java9-di-service-loader\com.packt.client>copy ..\com.packt.service.impl\sms-service.jar lib\sms-service.jar
        1 file(s) copied.

D:\java9di\java9-di-service-loader\com.packt.client>javac -d out --module-path lib src/module-info.java src/com/packt/client/ClientApplication.java

D:\java9di\java9-di-service-loader\com.packt.client>java --module-path out;lib --module com.packt.client/com.packt.client.ClientApplication
SMS has been sent to Recipient :: 1234567890 with Message :: Hello
```

Writing modular code using a command-line interface

As a tradition, let's create a simple module called helloApp, which will have a simple
message and will be required by another module called helloClient. Here, we will use a
command line interface to create and run the module.

Create a helloApp module folder named com.packt.helloapp and a package folder
named com\packt\helloapp:

```
mkdir com.packt.helloapp
mkdir com.packt.helloapp\com\packt\helloapp
```

Now, create a HelloApp.java component class under the package
name com.packt.helloapp\com\packt\helloapp and a modue-info.java file at root
folder com.packt.helloapp:

```
HelloApp.java
```

```
package com.packt.helloapp;

public class HelloApp {
  public String sayHelloJava() {
      return "Hello Java 9 Module System";
  }
}

module-info.java

module com.packt.helloapp {
 // define exports or requires.
 }
```

Now, we will create another module called `helloClient`. Create a `helloClient` module with the folder name `com.packt.hello.client` and a package with the folder name `com\packt\hello\client`:

```
mkdir com.packt.hello.client
mkdir com.packt.hello.client\com\packt\hello\client
```

Let's create another component class called `HelloClient.java` under the `com.packt.hello.client\com\packt\hello\client` package and create a `module-info.java` file at root folder `com.packt.hello.client`:

```
helloClient.java

package com.packt.hello.client;

public class HelloClient {
  public static void main (String arg[]) {
      //code
  }
}

module-info.java
module com.packt.hello.client {
 //define exports or requires
 }
```

Both modules are independent modules so are not dependent on each other. But if we want to use a method called `sayHelloJava()` in the `HelloClient` class, then we have to import the module, otherwise it will give a compile time error `package com.packt.helloapp is not visible`.

Defining dependency between modules

To use `HelloApp`, we need to export the package `com.packt.helloapp` from the `helloApp` module and include the `helloApp` module in the `helloClient` module:

```
module com.packt.helloapp {
    exports com.packt.helloapp;
}

module com.packt.hello.client {
    requires com.packt.helloapp;
}
```

From the preceding code, the first module descriptor, the `exports` keyword, indicates that packages are available to export to other modules. If a package is explicitly exported, then it is only accessible by other modules. If in a same module some packages are not exported, then it cannot be accessed by other modules.

The second module descriptor uses the `requires` keyword to indicate that the module is dependent on the `com.packt.helloapp` module, and this is called Dependency Injection in Java 9 Module.

Finally, the `HelloClient` class will be as follows:

```
HelloClient.java

package com.packt.hello.client;

import com.packt.HelloApp;

public class HelloClient {

  public static void main (String arg[]) {

    HelloApp helloApp = new HelloApp();
    System.out.println(helloApp.sayHelloJava());
  }

}
```

After creating two modules, the following will be the final tree structure:

```
C:\Windows\System32\cmd.exe

Microsoft Windows [Version 10.0.16299.64]
(c) 2017 Microsoft Corporation. All rights reserved.

C:\java9examples>tree /F
Folder PATH listing
Volume serial number is 74A2-791E
C:.
├───com.packt.hello.client
│       module-info.java
│
│   └───com
│       └───packt
│           └───hello
│               └───client
│                       HelloClient.java
└───com.packt.helloapp
        module-info.java

    └───com
        └───packt
            └───helloapp
                    HelloApp.java

C:\java9examples>
```

But wait, we only wrote the code and have not compiled and run it yet. Let's do that in the next section.

Compiling and running modules

Let's first compile the `HelloApp` module and then the `HelloClient` module. Before running the command, make sure that the Java 9 ClassPath is set. To compile module code, the following command needs to run:

```
javac -d output com.packt.helloapp\com\packt\helloapp\HelloApp.java
com.packt.helloapp\module-info.java
```

On successful compilation it will generate `HelloApp.class` and `module-info.class` into the output directory.

As our `HelloApp` module is required by the `HelloClient` module, we should generate the `com.packt.helloapp` module jar to include it in the `HelloClient` module. To create a jar in the `mlib` folder, run the following jar command:

```
jar -c -f mlib\com.packt.helloapp.jar -C output .
```

Now, remove the output directory by running the following command and again make an output directory for the second module:

```
rmdir /s output
```

In order to compile the `HelloClient` module, we need to provide a reference of `com.packt.hellpapp.jar` and `javac` commands and provide a way to pass `module-path` to refer to other modules. Here we pass the `mlib` directory as a module path. Without `module-path`, compilation of the `com.packt.hello.client` module is not possible:

```
javac --module-path mlib -d output com.packt.hello.client\module-info.java
javac --module-path mlib -d output
com.packt.hello.client\com\packt\hello\client\HelloClient.java
```

Now, let's run the module with the help of the following command:

```
java --module-path "mlib;output" -m
com.packt.hello.client/com.packt.hello.client.HelloClient
```

The output will be as follows:

```
C:\java9examples>java --module-path "mlib;output" -m com.packt.hello.client/com.packt.hello.client.HelloClient
Hello Java 9 Module System

C:\java9examples>
```

At the end of the preceding example, we learned how to create a module and define Dependency Injection in Java modules. The following diagram shows how one module is dependent on another:

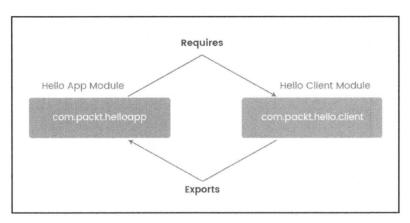

Summary

Here, the journey ends for Dependency Injection in Java 9. Let's summarize what we learned from this chapter. Firstly, we learned key features introduced in Java 9, such as Java Platform Module System, JShell, JLink tool, multi-release of JAR, Enhanced Stream API, Stack-Walking PI, Immutable collection methods, and HTTP 2.0.

Secondly, in Modular Frameworks in Java 9 section, we learned the meaning of modularity and the need of modular design in Java applications. We also learned how JPMS changes the earlier JDK into Modular JDK in detail.

After that we learned about an important element of modular systems, which is modules. We saw how module structure is defined with the help of different module descriptors and module types.

And lastly, we learned how to write simple modules using commands to understand how Dependency Injection works in Java 9 between modules.

In the next chapter, we will discuss concepts of Dependency Injection in Spring Framework in detail.

Dependency Injection with Spring

3

So far, we have learned why modularity is so important in writing cleaner and maintainable code. In `Chapter 1`, *Why Dependency Injection?*, we learned about the **Dependency Inversion Principle (DIP)**, **IoC** (a design methodology to implement DIP), and various design patterns to implement IoC. **Dependency Injection (DI)** is one of the design patterns to achieve IoC.

In the `Chapter 2`, *Dependency Injection in Java 9*, we learned how modular framework and DI are facilitated in Java 9. In this chapter, we will continue our journey to learn DI in Spring—one of the most popular and widely used frameworks to implement enterprise applications.

In this chapter, we will explore the following topics:

- A brief introduction to Spring framework
- Bean management in Spring
- How to achieve DI with Spring
- Auto wiring: he feature of resolving dependency automatically
- Annotation-based DI implementation
- DI implementation with Java-based configuration

A brief introduction to Spring framework

Spring is a lightweight and open source enterprise framework created way back in 2003. Modularity is the heart of Spring framework. Because of this, Spring can be used from the presentation layer to the persistence layer.

The good thing is, Spring doesn't force you to use Spring in all layers. For example, if you use Spring in the persistence layer, you are free to use any other framework in presentation of the controller layer.

Another good part of Spring is its **Plain Old Java Object** (**POJO**) model-based framework. Unlike other frameworks, Spring doesn't force your class to extend or implement any base class or interface of Spring API; however, Spring does provide a set of classes to use other frameworks, such as ORM frameworks, logging framework, Quartz timers, and other third-party libraries, which will help you to integrate those frameworks with Spring.

More on this: Spring allows you to change the similar framework without changing the code. For example, you can choose different persistence frameworks just by changing the configuration. This is also applicable to third-party API integration with Spring.

 Spring is a POJO-based framework; a servlet container is suffice to run your application and a fully-fledged application server is not required.

Spring framework architecture

Spring is a modular framework. This brings great flexibility to choosing the modules that you need instead of bringing all of them together in your code. Spring comprises around 20 modules that are logically grouped into the following layers:

- Core container layer
- Data access/integration layer
- Web layer
- Test layer
- Miscellaneous layer

Core container layer

Being a main part of the framework, the core container covers the following modules:

Spring core: As its name suggests, it provides core functionalities of the framework, including an IoC container and DI mechanism. An IoC container isolates the configuration and dependencies management from the application code.

Spring beans: This module provides the bean factory to create and manage the life cycle of beans (objects). It is a factory pattern implementation.

Spring context: This module is built on top of core and bean modules. Its entry point is to load the configuration and access the objects. On top of bean modules, the context module provides some additional features such as event propagation, creating context on the fly, internationalization, and so on.

Spring Expression Language (SpEL): This is an expression language to access and manipulate objects on the fly in JSP. It's an extension of **Expression Language (EL)** of JSP 2.1 specification. Using SpEL makes the JSP code cleaner, more readable, and maintainable. Major benefits of using SpEL are:

- The setting of and getting properties' values of objects with ease
- It can directly invoke controller methods to get the data
- It's used to retrieve objects directly from Spring's application context (IoC container)
- It supports various list operations such as projection, selection, iteration, and aggregation
- It provides logical and arithmetic operations

Data access/integration layer

Spring data access and the integration layer is used for data manipulation and other integration. It covers the following modules:

- **Transaction**: This module helps maintain transactions in a programmatic and declarative manner. This module supports ORM and JDBC modules.
- **Object XML mapping (OXM)**: This module provides abstraction of Object/XML processing, which can be used by various OXM implementation such as JAXB, XMLBeans, and so on, to integrate with Spring.
- **Object Relationship Mapping (ORM)**: Spring doesn't provide its own ORM framework; instead it facilitates integration with ORM frameworks such as Hibernate, JPA, JDO, and so on, with this module.
- **Java Database Connectivity (JDBC)**: This module provides all low-level boilerplate code to deal with JDBC. You can use it to interact with databases with standard JDBC API.
- **Java Messaging Service (JMS)**: This module supports integration of messaging systems in Spring.

Spring web layer

Spring web layer is used to create web-based applications. It is comprised of the following modules:

- **Web**: This module provides basic web-related features such as multipart file upload (with the help of Spring custom tags in JSP). It is also responsible for initialization of IoC containers in web context.
- **Servlet:** This module provides implementation of Spring MVC (Model View Controller) for web-based applications. It provides clear separation of views (presentation layer) from models (business logic), and controls the flow between them with controllers.
- **Portlet:** This module provides MVC implementation for a portlet, and it is mainly used in portal environments.

Spring test

This provides support for unit and integration testing with various unit-testing frameworks, such as JUnit and TestNg. We will see how to perform unit testing with Spring in upcoming sections in this chapter, so keep reading.

Miscellaneous

Some additional modules are also part of the Spring framework:

- **Aspect and AOP:** These modules provide a facility to apply common logic (called *concerns* in AOP terminology) across multiple application layers dynamically
- **Instrumentation:** This module provides a class instrumentation facility and class loader implementation
- **Messaging:** This module provides support for **Streaming Text-Oriented Messaging Protocol** (**STOMP**) for communicating with various STOMP-based clients

Bean management in Spring container

When any software application is being executed, a set of objects are created and interact with each other to achieve specific business goals. Being a POJO-based programming model, the Spring framework treats all the objects of classes in your application as POJO or beans (in a Spring-friendly way).

These objects or beans should be independent in a manner that they can be re-used or changed without causing the ripple effect of changing others. Being loosely coupled this way, it also provides the benefit of doing testing without much worry of any dependency.

Spring provides an IoC container, which is used to automate the process of supplying external dependency to your class. You need to give instruction (in the form of configuration) about your client and dependencies. Spring will manage and resolve all your dependencies at runtime. Moreover, Spring provides a facility to keep availability of your dependencies at various application scopes, such as request, session, application, and so on.

It's essential to understand how Spring manages the life cycle (the process of creating, managing, and destroying) of objects before getting an idea about injecting dependency. In Spring, all these responsibilities are performed by the Spring IoC container.

Spring IoC container

In Spring, the `org.springframework.beans.factory.BeanFactory` interface defines the basic IoC container, while the `org.springframework.context.ApplicationContext` interface represents an advanced IoC container. `ApplicationContext` is a super set of `BeanFactory`. It provides some additional enterprise-level functionalities on top of basic IoC features by `BeanFactory`.

To cater for different types of applications, Spring provides various implementations of `ApplicationContext` out of the box. For standalone applications, you can use the `FileSystemXmlApplicationContext` or `ClassPathXmlApplicationContext` class. They are both implementations of `ApplicationConext`.

While working with Spring, you need to pass one XML file as an entry point for these containers. This file is called the **Spring Application Context file**. When the Spring container starts, it loads this XML file and starts configuring your beans (either with XML-based bean definition in this file, or annotation-based definition in your POJO Java class).

- `FileSystemXmlApplicationContext`: This container loads the Spring XML file and processes it. You need to give the full path of the XML file.
- `ClassPathXmlApplicationContext`: This container works similarly to `FileSystemXmlApplicationContext`; however, it assumes that the Spring XML file is available in `CLASSPATH`. You do not need to pass a root-level path for it.
- `WebXmlApplicationContext`: This container is generally used within web applications.

Spring's IoC container is responsible for instantiating, configuring, maintaining, and accumulating the beans (objects in your application). You need to provide configuration metadata about the objects you want to assemble with the IoC container. The following diagram depicts a high-level flow of how the IoC container gets this work done:

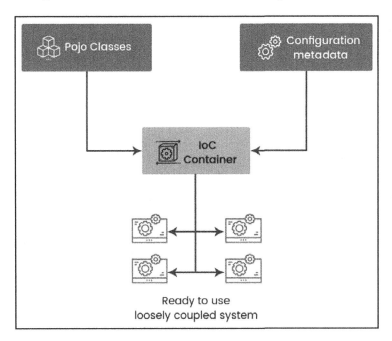

We provide **Pojo Classes** (or bean definitions) and **Configuration metadata** (set of instructions) as an input. The Spring IoC container will create and manage the objects (or beans) in a way that they produce a ready-to-use system. In short, an IoC container performs all low-level tasks (of managing beans and dependencies) so that you can write business logic in your POJO class.

Configuration

You need to give instructions to Spring's container about how you want to configure your beans based on your application needs. These instructions should be in the form of configuration metadata, and they should tell the following things to the IoC container:

- **Instantiation**: How to create the objects from bean definitions.
- **Lifespan**: Till what time these objects are available.
- **Dependencies**: Do they need someone else?

Spring provides a great amount of flexibility, even in defining the configuration metadata. You can supply it to the IoC container in the following three ways:

- **XML format:** One or more entries with configuration metadata about beans in Spring's Application Context (XML) file.
- **Java annotation:** Put the configuration metadata in the form of an annotation in a Java class.
- **pure Java code:** From version 3.0, Spring started support of defining configuration with Java code. You can define beans outside of your application classes by using Java rather than XML files.

When the Spring application starts, it will load the application context (XML) file first. This file looks as follows:

```xml
<?xml version="1.0" encoding="UTF-8"?>
<beans xmlns="http://www.springframework.org/schema/beans"
    xmlns:xsi="http://www.w3.org/2001/XMLSchema-instance"
    xsi:schemaLocation="http://www.springframework.org/schema/beans
        http://www.springframework.org/schema/beans/spring-beans.xsd">

    <!-- All your bean and its configuration metadata goes here -->
    <bean id="..." class="...">
    </bean>
</beans>
```

This file must be present for both XML-based and annotation-based configuration metadata. In the case of XML-based configuration, you need to define your bean with the `<bean>` element under top-level `<beans>` elements in this file. One or multiple `<bean>` entries can be defined. The configuration metadata will go along with the `<bean>` element.

In the preceding bean definition, the `id` attribute defines the identity of that bean. The container will use it to point out the specific bean, so it must be unique. While the `class` attribute defines the type of bean, you need to give its fully qualified class name here.

Each bean is associated with an actual object through the `class` attribute. You can define beans for any type of class, such as your custom service layer classes, DAO layer classes, presentation classes, and so on. Spring's container will use the `class` attribute to instantiate the objects, and it applies the configuration metadata associated with the corresponding `<bean>` element.

In case of annotation-based configuration, your metadata will be defined to actual Java classes and in this (XML) file; you need to just specify the base package name with the `<context:component-scan base-package="org.example"/>` element. We will see more on this in an upcoming section, *Annotation-based DI*, in this chapter.

Containers in action

To understand the flow of Spring-based applications with ease, we will take an example of standalone application containers: `ClassPathXmlApplicationContext`, or `FileSystemXmlApplicationContext`. The whole process of dealing with Spring comprises the following three steps:

- Defining POJOs
- Creating application context (XML) files with configuration metadata
- Initializing the container

Defining POJOs: As we have seen in previous sections of this chapter, Spring considers each object in your application as a POJO. So, first you need to define POJOs. We will use simple examples to understand the concepts as per the following snippet:

```
package com.packet.spring.contaner.check;
public class Car{
    public void showType(){
        System.out.println("This is patrol car..");
    }
}
```

Providing application context (XML) files: Create one XML file and name it `application-context.xml`. For the sake of simplicity, we use XML-based configuration metadata. We will see another two ways (annotation-based and Java code-based) of setting configuration metadata in upcoming sections.

Define `<bean>` for each of your module classes along with their configuration metadata in the application context file (`application-context.xml`), as per the following snippet:

```
<?xml version="1.0" encoding="UTF-8"?>
<beans xmlns="http://www.springframework.org/schema/beans"
    xmlns:xsi="http://www.w3.org/2001/XMLSchema-instance"
    xsi:schemaLocation="http://www.springframework.org/schema/beans
        http://www.springframework.org/schema/beans/spring-beans.xsd">

    <!-- All your bean and its configuration metadata goes here -->
    <bean id="myCar" class="com.packet.spring.contaner.check.Car">
    </bean>
</beans>
```

We have defined `<bean>` for our POJO –`Car` with `id="myCar"`. The Spring container uses this ID to get the object of the `Car` bean.

Initializing container: In case of a web-based application, the container (`WebXmlApplicationContext`) will be initialized by a web listener when an application is loaded into the servlet container. In case of a standalone application, you need to initialize the containers (`ClassPathXmlApplicationContext` or `FileSystemXmlApplicationContext`) with Java code, as per the following snippet:

```
ApplicationContext context = new
ClassPathXmlApplicationContext("application-context.xml");
```

`ClassPathXmlApplicationContext` and `FileSystemXmlApplicationContext` take resource String as an input parameter in the constructor. This resource string represents the application context (XML) file from the classpath (in the preceding snippet), or from the local filesystem (in case of the `FileSystemXmlApplicationContext` container).

There are other overloaded constructors of `ClassPathXmlApplicationContext` and `FileSystemXmlApplicationContext` containers, such as a no-argument constructor and string array argument constructor, which is used to load more than one application context (XML) file.

Soon after the Spring container is loaded into memory, it processes the application context (XML) file and creates the objects for corresponding `<bean>` definition. You can get the instance of your bean with the help of a container, as per the following snippet:

```
// create and configure beans
ApplicationContext context = new
ClassPathXmlApplicationContext("application-context.xml");

// retrieve configured instance
Car carObj = context.getBean("myCar");

// use configured instance
carObj.showType();
```

When you call the `getBean` method, the container internally calls its constructor to create the object, which is equivalent to calling the `new()` operator. This is how Spring's IoC container creates, maintains, and assembles the objects corresponding to each `<bean>` definition in Spring's application context(XML) file.

 By default, Spring creates the object of each `<bean>` element with a Singleton fashion. It means a container creates and holds just one object of each `<bean>` unless you explicitly tell it not to. When you ask a container for the object of `<bean>` with the `getBean()` method, it gives the reference of the same object every time after creating it the first time.

When a container creates the object corresponding to the `<bean>` definition, you do not need to implement any specific interface, or extend any class or code in a specific way. Simply specifying the `class` attribute of `<bean>` is suffice. Spring is capable enough to create an object of any type.

Dependency Injection (DI) in Spring

After getting an idea of how Spring manages bean life cycle, next we will learn how Spring provides and maintains the dependencies in your application.

DI is a process of providing the dependent objects to other objects that need it. In Spring, the container supplies the dependencies. The flow of creating and managing the dependencies is inverted from client to container. That is the reason we call it an **IoC container**.

A Spring IoC container uses the Dependency Injection (DI) mechanism to provide the dependency at runtime. In `Chapter 1`, *Why Dependency Injection?*, we saw various DI types such as constructor, setter method, and interface-based. Let's see how we can implement the constructor and setter-based DI through Spring's IoC container.

Constructor-based DI

Constructor-based dependency is generally used where you want to pass mandatory dependencies before the object is instantiated. It's provided by a container through a constructor with different arguments, and each represents dependency.

When a container starts, it checks wheather any constructor-based DI is defined for `<bean>`. It will create the dependency objects first, and then pass them to the current object's constructor. We will understand this by taking the classic example of using logging. It is good practice to put the log statement at various places in code to trace the flow of execution.

Let's say you have an `EmployeeService` class where you need to put a log in each of its methods. To achieve separation of concern, you put the log functionality in a separated class called `Logger`. To make sure the `EmployeeService` and `Logger` are independent and loosely coupled, you need to inject the `Logger` object into the `EmployeeService` object. Let's see how to achieve this by constructor-based injection:

```java
public class EmployeeService {
    private Logger log;
    //Constructor
     public EmployeeService(Logger log) {
         this.log = log;
     }
    //Service method.
    public void showEmployeeName() {
       log.info("showEmployeeName method is called ....");
       log.debug("This is Debuggin point");
       log.error("Some Exception occured here ...");
    }

}

public class Logger {
   public void info(String msg){
        System.out.println("Logger INFO: "+msg);
    }
   public void debug(String msg){
```

```
        System.out.println("Logger DEBUG: "+msg);
    }
  public void error(String msg){
        System.out.println("Logger ERROR: "+msg);
    }
}


public class DIWithConstructorCheck {

  public static void main(String[] args) {
    ApplicationContext springContext = new
ClassPathXmlApplicationContext("application-context.xml");
    EmployeeService employeeService = (EmployeeService)
springContext.getBean("employeeService");
    employeeService.showEmployeeName();

  }
}
```

As per the preceding code, when these objects are configured with Spring, the `EmployeeService` object expects the Spring container to inject the object of `Logger` through the constructor. To achieve this, you need to set the configuration metadata as per the following snippet:

```
<?xml version="1.0" encoding="UTF-8"?>
<beans xmlns="http://www.springframework.org/schema/beans"
    xmlns:xsi="http://www.w3.org/2001/XMLSchema-instance"
    xsi:schemaLocation="http://www.springframework.org/schema/beans
        http://www.springframework.org/schema/beans/spring-beans.xsd">

    <!-- All your bean and its configuration metadata goes here -->
    <bean id="employeeService"
class="com.packet.spring.constructor.di.EmployeeService">
        <constructor-arg ref="logger"/>
    </bean>

    <bean id="logger" class="com.packet.spring.constructor.di.Logger">
    </bean>
</beans>
```

In the preceding configuration, the `Logger` bean is injected into the `employee` bean through the `constructor-arg` element. It has a `ref` attribute, which is used to point to other beans with a matching `id` value. This configuration instructs Spring to pass the object of `Logger` into the constructor of the `EmployeeService` bean.

You can put the <bean> definition in any order here. Spring will create the objects of <bean> based on need, and not as per the order they are defined here.

For more than one constructor argument, you can pass additional <constructor-arg> elements. The order is not important as far as the object type (class attribute of referred bean) is not ambiguous.

Spring also supports DI with primitive constructor arguments. Spring provides the facility to pass the primitive values in a constructor from an application context (XML) file. Let's say you want to create an object of the Camera class with a default value, as per the following snippet:

```
public class Camera {
   private int resolution;
   private String mode;
   private boolean smileShot;
   //Constructor.
   public Camera(int resolution, String mode, boolean smileShot) {
      this.resolution = resolution;
      this.mode = mode;
      this.smileShot = smileShot;
   }
   //Public method
   public void showSettings() {
      System.out.println("Resolution:"+resolution+"px mode:"+mode+"
smileShot:"+smileShot);
   }
}
```

The Camera class has three properties: resolution, mode, and smileShot. Its constructor takes three primitive arguments to create a camera object with default values. You need to give configuration metadata in the following way, so that Spring can create instances of the Camera object with default primitive values:

```
<bean id="camera" class="com.packet.spring.constructor.di.Camera">
      <constructor-arg type="int" value="12" />
      <constructor-arg type="java.lang.String" value="normal" />
      <constructor-arg type="boolean" value="false" />
</bean>
```

We pass three `<constructor-arg>` elements under `<bean>`, corresponding to each constructor argument. Since these are primitive, Spring has no idea about its type while passing the value. So, we need to explicitly pass the `type` attribute, which defines the type of primitive constructor argument.

In case of primitive also, there is no fixed order to pass the value of the constructor argument, as long as the type is not ambiguous. In previous cases, all three types are different, so Spring intelligently picks up the right constructor argument, no matter which order you pass them.

Now we are adding one more attribute to the `Camera` class called `flash`, as per the following snippet:

```
//Constructor.
  public Camera(int resolution, String mode, boolean smileShot, boolean
flash) {
    this.resolution = resolution;
    this.mode = mode;
    this.smileShot = smileShot;
    this.flash = flash;
  }
```

In this case, the constructor arguments `smileShot` and `flash` are of the same type (Boolean), and you pass the constructor argument value from XML configuration as per the following snippet:

```
<constructor-arg type="java.lang.String" value="normal"/>
<constructor-arg type="boolean" value="true" />
<constructor-arg type="int" value="12" />
<constructor-arg type="boolean" value="false" />
```

In the preceding scenario, Spring will pick up the following:

- int value for resolution
- String value for mode
- First Boolean value (true) in sequence for first Boolean argument—`smileShot`
- Second Boolean value (false) in sequence for second Boolean argument—flash

In short, for similar types in constructor arguments, Spring will pick the first value that comes in the sequence. So sequence does matter in this case.

This may lead to logical errors, as you are passing wrong values to the right argument. To avoid such accidental mistakes, Spring provides the facility to define a zero-based index in the `<constructor-arg>` element, as per the following snippet:

```
<constructor-arg type="java.lang.String" value="normal"
index="1"/>
<constructor-arg type="boolean" value="true" index="3"/>
<constructor-arg type="int" value="12" index="0"/>
<constructor-arg type="boolean" value="false" index="2"/>
```

This is more readable and less error prone. Now Spring will pick up the last value (with `index=2`) for `smileShot`, and the second value (with `index=3`) for `flash` arguments. Index attributes resolves the ambiguity of two constructor arguments having the same type.

If the `type` you defined in `<constructor-arg>` is not compatible with the actual type of constructor argument in that index, then Spring will raise an error. So just make sure about this while using index attribute.

Setter-based DI

Setter-based DI is generally used for optional dependencies. In case of setter-based DI, the container first creates an instance of your bean, either by calling a no-argument constructor or static `factory` method. It then passes the said dependencies through each setter method. Dependencies injected through the setter method can be re-injected or changed at a later stage of application.

We will understand setter-based DI with the following code base:

```
public class DocumentBase {
  private DocFinder docFinder;
 //Setter method to inject dependency.
 public void setDocFinder(DocFinder docFinder) {
    this.docFinder = docFinder;
  }
  public void performSearch() {
    this.docFinder.doFind();
  }

}

public class DocFinder {
  public void doFind() {
    System.out.println(" Finding in Document Base ");
  }
```

```
  }

public class DIWithSetterCheck {
  public static void main(String[] args) {
    ApplicationContext springContext = new
ClassPathXmlApplicationContext("application-context.xml");
    DocumentBase docBase = (DocumentBase) springContext.getBean("docBase");
    docBase.performSearch();
  }
}
```

The `DocumentBase` class depends on `DocFinder`, and we are passing it through the `setter` method. You need to define the configuration metadata for Spring, as per the following snippet:

```
<bean id="docBase" class="com.packet.spring.setter.di.DocumentBase">
    <property name="docFinder" ref="docFinder" />
</bean>

<bean id="docFinder" class="com.packet.spring.setter.di.DocFinder">
</bean>
```

Setter-based DI can be defined through the `<property>` element under `<bean>`. The `name` attribute denotes the name of the `setter` name. In our case, the `name` attribute of the `property` element is `docFinder`, so Spring will call the `setDocFinder` method to inject the dependency. The pattern to find the `setter` method is to prepend `set` and make the first character capital.

The `name` attribute of the `<property>` element is case-sensitive. So, if you set the name to `docfinder`, Spring will try to call the `setDocfinder` method and will show an error.

Just like constructor DI, Setter DI also supports supplying the value for primitives, as per the following snippet:

```
<bean id="docBase" class="com.packet.spring.setter.di.DocumentBase">
    <property name="buildNo" value="1.2.6" />
</bean>
```

Since the `setter` method takes only one argument, there is no scope of argument ambiguity. Whatever value you are passing here, Spring will convert it to an actual primitive type of the `setter` method parameter. If it's not compatible, it will show an error.

Spring DI with the factory method

So far, we have seen that the Spring container takes care of creating the instances of bean. In some scenarios, you need to take control of creating an instance of bean with custom code. Spring supports this feature with the help of the factory method.

You can write your custom logic to create the instance in the factory method, and just instruct Spring to use it. When Spring encounters such instructions, it will call the factory method to create the instance. So, the factory method is kind of a callback function.

There are two flavors of the factory method: static, and instance (non-static).

Static factory method

When you want to encapsulate the logic of creating the instance in a static way to custom methods, you can use a static factory method. In this case, Spring will use the Class attribute of <bean> to call the factory method and generate instances. Let's understand this by looking at the following example:

```
public class SearchableFactory {
  private static SearchableFactory searchableFactory;
  //Static factory method to get instance of Searchable Factory.
  public static SearchableFactory getSearchableFactory() {
    if(searchableFactory == null) {
      searchableFactory = new SearchableFactory();
    }
    System.out.println("Factory method is used: getSearchableFactory() ");
    return searchableFactory;
  }
}


public class DIWithFactoryCheck {
  public static void main(String[] args) {
    ApplicationContext springContext = new
ClassPathXmlApplicationContext("application-context.xml");
    SearchableFactory searchableFactory =
(SearchableFactory)springContext.getBean("searchableFactory");
  }
}
```

In the previous code snippet, the `SearchableFactory` class has one static method, `getSearchableFactory`, which returns the object of the same class. This behaves as a `factory` method. The preceding code can be configured in Spring, as per the following snippet:

```
<bean id="searchableFactory"
class="com.packet.spring.factory.di.SearchableFactory" factory-
method="getSearchableFactory">
</bean>
```

In the previous configuration, Spring will always use the `getSearchableFactory` method to create the instance of bean irrespective of any scope.

Instance (non-static) factory method

You can use an instance `factory` method to shift the control of creating the instance from a container to your custom object. The only difference between an instance `factory` method and a static `factory` method is that the former can only be invoked with an instance of bean. Let's understand this by taking the following example:

```
public class Employee {
  private String type;
  public Employee(String type) {
    this.type = type;
  }
  public void showType() {
    System.out.println("Type is :"+type);
  }
}

public class Developer extends Employee {
  public Developer(String type) {
    super(type);
  }
}

public class Manager extends Employee {
  public Manager(String type) {
    super(type);
  }
}

//Factory Bean who has Factory method.
public class EmployeeService {
  //Instance Factory method
```

```
  public Employee getEmployee(String type) {
    Employee employee = null;
    if("developer".equalsIgnoreCase(type)) {
      employee = new Developer("developer");
    }else if("manager".equalsIgnoreCase(type)) {
      employee = new Manager("manager");
    }
    return employee;
  }
}

public class SalaryService {
  private Employee employee;
  public void setEmployee(Employee employee) {
    this.employee = employee;
  }
  public void showEmployeeType() {
    if(this.employee !=null) {
      this.employee.showType();
    }
  }
}

public class DIWithInstanceFactoryCheck {
  public static void main(String[] args) {
    ApplicationContext springContext = new
ClassPathXmlApplicationContext("application-context.xml");
    SalaryService salaryService =
(SalaryService)springContext.getBean("salaryService");
    salaryService.showEmployeeType();
  }
}
```

Employee is a generic class that has a type instance variable. Developer and Manager extend Employee, and they pass the type in the constructor. EmployeeService is a class that has a factory method: getEmployee. This method takes a String argument, and generates either Developer or Manager objects.

These objects can be configured in Spring as per the following snippet:

```
<bean id="employeeService"
class="com.packet.spring.factory.di.EmployeeService">
</bean>
<bean id="developerBean" factory-method="getEmployee" factory-
bean="employeeService">
    <constructor-arg value="developer"></constructor-arg>
</bean>
```

```
<bean id="salaryService"
class="com.packet.spring.factory.di.SalaryService">
      <property name="employee" ref="developerBean"/>
</bean>
```

The `employeeService` is defined with normal bean definition. The `developerBean` is defined with `factory-method` and `factory-bean` attributes. The `factory-bean` attribute represents the reference of bean in which the `factory` method is defined.

In previous cases, `developerBean` is created by calling the `factory` method `getEmployee` on bean `employeeService`. The argument passed through `<constructor-arg>` to `developerBean` actually goes to the `factory` method. You will also notice that we haven't defined a `class` attribute for `developerBean`, because when `factory-bean` is defined for bean, Spring will consider the class as a returned type from the `factory` method (defined in factory bean), rather than considering the bean's class.

This way, `developerBean` is a kind of virtual bean that is generated by the `factory` method of another class. Lastly, we have created `salaryService`, and passed the `developerBean` as a setter injection. When you execute this code, it shows the type as a `developer`. This is how we can use the instance `factory` method.

 The type of class returned by the `factory` method need not be the same as the class in which the `factory` method is defined. If you have used a different class, you need to cast with the class that is being returned from the `factory` method, while calling the `getBean()` method of `ApplicationContext`.

By default, Spring uses `singleton` scope for each of the beans. It means Spring will create just one object of each bean. For other scopes such as `prototype`, Spring creates a new instance every time you make a call to the `getBean` method. But if you specify which `factory` method, Spring will call the `factory` method to get the object all the time.

In our case, we are using the `factory` method to make sure Spring creates just one object of our bean, irrespective of the bean's scope. This is just one example. This way you can use the `factory` method with any custom logic while creating the instance. It basically encapsulates the object instantiation process.

Auto-wiring in Spring

So far, we have learned how to define configuration metadata along with `<bean>` to set the dependencies. How good would it be if everything was settled down without giving any instruction in the form of configuration? That is a cool idea, and the good news is that Spring supports it.

This feature is called autowire (in Spring terminology), which automates the process of binding relations between beans. This greatly reduces the effort of providing configuration metadata at either properties or constructor arguments.

The autowire feature can be enabled in XML-based configuration metadata by defining the `autowire` attribute of the `<bean>` element. It can be specified with the following three modes: name, type, and constructor. By default, autowire is set off for all beans.

Auto-wiring by name

As its name suggests, in this mode, Spring does the wiring of beans by name. Spring looks for beans with the same name (ID) as the property that needs to be autowired. In other words, dependencies are auto-bound with the bean that has the same name (value of ID attribute) as the property name. Let's understand this by looking at the following example:

```java
public class UserService {
  public void getUserDetail() {
    System.out.println(" This is user detail ");
  }
}

public class AccountService {
  private UserService userService=null;
  public void setUserService(UserService userService) {
    this.userService = userService;
  }
  //Setter DI method.
  public void processUserAccount() {
    if(userService !=null) {
      userService.getUserDetail();
    }
  }
}

public class DIAutoWireCheck {
  public static void main(String[] args) {
    ApplicationContext springContext = new
```

```
ClassPathXmlApplicationContext("application-context.xml");
    AccountService accountService =
(AccountService)springContext.getBean("accountService");
    accountService.processUserAccount();
  }
}
```

In the preceding code, `AccountService` depends on `UserService`. `AccountService` has a setter method through which Spring will inject the dependency of `UserService`. The preceding scenario can be configured in Spring as follows:

```
<bean id="userService" class="com.packet.spring.autowire.di.UserService">
</bean>
<bean id="accountService"
class="com.packet.spring.autowire.di.AccountService" autowire="byName">
</bean>
```

In typical setter-based DI configuration, we would have used the `<property>` element for the `accountService` bean, and defined the `ref` attribute to refer to the `userService` bean. But in previous cases, we haven't used the property element, and `userService` is still injected into `accountService` by Spring.

This magic is done by the attribute `autowire="byName"`. How does this work? Well, when Spring reads this attribute in `<bean>`, it will try to search the bean with the same `name` (`id`) as the property (setter method) name. If found, it will inject that bean to the current bean's setter method on which the `autowire` attribute is defined.

In our case, `autowire="byName"` is set on the `accountService` bean, which has setter method `setUserService` to set the instance of `userService`. Spring will try to find any bean with the ID `userService` and, if found, it will inject the instance of the `userService` bean through this setter method.

In this case, the autowire happens with the name of the setter method instead of the property name. For example, if you set the setter method name as `setUserService1`, Spring will try to find the bean with `id=userService1`, irrespective of the actual property name.

Auto-wiring by type

In this mode, Spring does binding of beans based on type. Here, the type means the `class` attribute of `<bean>`. Spring looks for the bean with the same type as the property that needs to be autowired. In other words, dependencies are auto bound with the bean having the same type.

If more than one bean of the same type exists, Spring shows exception. If Spring doesn't find the bean with a matching type, nothing happens; simply, the property will not be set. Let's understand this by looking at the following example:

```
public class EmailService {
  public void sendEmail() {
    System.out.println(" Sending Email ..!! ");
  }
}

public class HRService {
  private EmailService emailService = null;
  //Setter DI method.
  public void setEmailService(EmailService emailService) {
    this.emailService = emailService;
  }
public void initiateSeparation() {
    //Business logic for sepration process
    if(emailService !=null) {
      emailService.sendEmail();
    }
  }
}
```

In the preceding code, `HRService` depends on `EmailService`. `HRService` has a setter method through which Spring will inject the dependency of `EmailService`. Previous scenarios can be configured in Spring as follows:

```
<!-- Example of autowire byType -->
<bean id="emailService" class="com.packet.spring.autowire.di.EmailService">
</bean>
<bean id="hrService" class="com.packet.spring.autowire.di.HRService"
autowire="byType">
</bean>
```

When Spring reads the `autowire="byType"` attribute in the `hrService` bean, it will try to search the bean with the same type as the property of `hrService`. Spring expects just one such bean. If found, it will inject that bean.

 Since this is autowire by type, Spring relies on the type of property to inject the dependency, and not on the name of the setter method. Spring only expects that the method should take the reference of dependency as a parameter to set it with the property of the bean.

Auto-wiring by constructor

This mode is identical to autowire by type. The only difference is, in this case, the autowire happens to constructor arguments rather than properties of the bean. When Spring encounters autowire with constructor mode, it will try to search and bind the bean's constructor argument with exactly one bean of the same type. Let's understand this by looking at the following example:

```
public class StudentService {
  public void getStudentDetail() {
    System.out.println(" This is Student details.. ");
  }
}

public class ExamService {
  private StudentService studentService;
  private String examServiceType;
  public ExamService(StudentService studentService, String examServiceType)
{
    this.studentService=studentService;
    this.examServiceType = examServiceType;
  }
  public void getExamDetails() {
    if(studentService !=null) {
      //Business logic to get exam details.
      studentService.getStudentDetail();
    }
  }
}
```

In the preceding code, `ExamService` depends on `StudentService`. `ExamService` has a constructor through which Spring will inject the dependency of `StudentService`. The previous scenario can be configured in Spring as follows:

```
<!-- Example of autowire by Constructor -->
<bean id="studentService"
class="com.packet.spring.autowire.di.StudentService">
 </bean>
<bean id="examService" class="com.packet.spring.autowire.di.ExamService"
autowire="constructor">
    <constructor-arg value="Science Exam"/>
</bean>
```

When Spring scans the attribute `autowire="constructor"` for the bean `examService`, it will search and inject any bean with the same type as `examService`'s constructor. In our case, we are using one constructor argument of the `StudentService` class, so Spring will inject the instance of the `studentService` bean, which we defined in the previous XML file.

Similar to autowire by type mode, if there is more than one bean with a matching type to the constructor argument type, Spring will throw an error. Along with `autowire = constructor` mode, you can still pass any additional arguments through the `<constructor-arg>` element shown in the previous configuration. If we hadn't used autowire here, we would have passed the `studentService` with the `<constructor-arg>` element.

In spite of the preceding advantages, the autowire feature should be used with a little caution. Following are the points you need to take into consideration while using it:

- Autowire can't be applied to primitive types.
- In case there are multiple beans of the same type, it will cause errors while using autowire by type and constructor, though there are options to avoid this.
- Since autowiring happens silently by Spring, sometimes it's difficult to find the logical issue when there are plenty of beans defined in the Spring application context files.
- People still prefer explicit mapping rather than autowiring, because explicit mapping is somewhat more accurate, clear, and more readable as well.

Annotation-based DI

From the beginning, the most common way of defining configuration in Spring has been XML-based. But when the complexity grew and navigation of beans became exhausted in the jungle of angle brackets, there was a demand for a second option to define configuration. As a result, Spring started support for annotation.

Annotation-based configuration is an alternate of XML-based configuration, and it relies on bytecode metadata. Spring started support for annotation with version 2.5. With annotation, the configuration moves from an XML to component class. Annotation can be declared on classes, methods, or at field level.

Let's understand the process of defining configuration through annotation. We will first understand this process through XML configuration, and then will gradually move to annotation-based configuration in the following sections.

DI through XML configuration

It's always good to start with the most common option. So first, we will take an example of pure XML-based configuration, as per the following snippet:

```
public class Professor {
  private String name;
  //Constructor
  public Professor() {
    System.out.println("Object of Professor is created");
  }
  public String getName() {
    return name;
  }
  public void setName(String name) {
    this.name = name;
  }
}

public class Subject {
  private Professor professor;
  public Subject() {
    System.out.println("Object of Subject is created");
  }
  //Setter injection method
  public void setProfessor(Professor professor) {
    System.out.println("setting the professor through setter method
injection ");
```

```
      this.professor = professor;
    }
    public void taughtBy() {
      if(professor !=null) {
        System.out.println("This subject is taught by "+professor.getName());
      }
    }
  }
}
public class DIAutoWireCheck {
  public static void main(String[] args) {
    ApplicationContext springContext = new
ClassPathXmlApplicationContext("application-context.xml");
    Subject subject = (Subject)springContext.getBean("subject");
    subject.taughtBy();
  }
}
```

In the previous code snippet, the `Subject` class depends on `Professor`. The object of the `Professor` class is injected into `Subject` through the setter injection. The XML-based configuration can be done with Spring as follows:

```
<bean id="professor" class="com.packet.spring.annotation.di.Professor">
    <property name="name" value="Nilang" />
</bean>
<bean id="subject" class="com.packet.spring.annotation.di.Subject">
    <property name="professor" ref="professor" />
</bean>
```

The object of the `Professor` bean will be created followed by setting the `name` property through the setter injection. Since the `name` property is primitive, we directly gave the value. Once the object of the `professor` bean is ready, it's injected into the object of the `subject` bean through the setter injection. To recall, in XML-based configuration, the setter injection can be performed by the `ref` attribute of the `<property>` element. Once you run this code, you will get output similar to the following:

```
...
INFO: Loading XML bean definitions from class path resource [application-
context.xml]
Object of Professor is created
Object of Subject is created
setting the professor through setter method injection
This subject is taught by Nilang
```

This is typical XML-based metadata, and we want to convert it into annotation-based configuration. The first annotation we will use in the previous example is `@Autowired`. It works similarly to its XML counterpart, `autowire`. It can be configured at field, constructor, and method level.

Defining annotation

Let's define `@Autowired` for the previous example. Our goal is to remove the XML configuration `<property name="professor" ref="professor" />` for the `subject` bean with the `@Autowired` annotation. Let's modify a `setter` method of the `Subject` class and Spring application (XML) context file, as follows:

```
//Updated setter injection method
  @Autowired
  public void setProfessor(Professor professor) {
    System.out.println("setting the professor through setter method
injection ");
    this.professor = professor;
  }

//Updated XML configuration
<bean id="professor" class="com.packet.spring.annotation.di.Professor">
    <property name="name" value="Nilang" />
</bean>
<bean id="subject" class="com.packet.spring.annotation.di.Subject">
</bean>
```

We are expected to auto-inject the object of `Professor` into `subject`, since we used the `@Autowired` annotation. When you run this code, you will get output similar to the following:

```
INFO: Loading XML bean definitions from class path resource [application-
context.xml]
Object of Professor is created
Object of Subject is created
```

Quick observation: only objects of `Professor` and `Subject` beans are created, and no setter is called. In spite of using the `@Autowired` annotation, dependency is not injected automatically. This has happened because, without being processed, annotations do nothing at all. It's like electronic equipment without being plugged in. You can't do anything with it.

By declaring configurations with annotations in the Java class, how does Spring know about it? This should be your first question when we talk about annotation-based DI. The answer is, we need to let Spring know about the annotation we defined, so that Spring can use it to get this work done.

Activating annotation-based configuration

Annotation-based configuration is not turned on by default. You need to enable it by defining the <context:annotation-config/> element in application context (XML) files. When Spring reads this element, it activates the actions for all annotations defined in beans in the same application context where this element is defined. In other words, Spring will activate the annotation on all the beans defined in the current application context where the <context:annotation-config /> element is defined.

Let's update the configuration and rerun the previous code. You will get output similar to the following:

```
// Updated Configuration
<beans xmlns="http://www.springframework.org/schema/beans"
    xmlns:xsi="http://www.w3.org/2001/XMLSchema-instance"
    xmlns:context="http://www.springframework.org/schema/context"
    xsi:schemaLocation="http://www.springframework.org/schema/beans
        http://www.springframework.org/schema/beans/spring-beans.xsd
        http://www.springframework.org/schema/context
        http://www.springframework.org/schema/context/spring-context.xsd">
    <context:annotation-config />
    <bean id="professor" class="com.packet.spring.annotation.di.Professor">
      <property name="name" value="Nilang" />
    </bean>
    <bean id="subject" class="com.packet.spring.annotation.di.Subject">
    </bean>
</beans>

//Output
...
INFO: Loading XML bean definitions from class path resource [application-
context.xml]
Object of Professor is created
Object of Subject is created
setting the professor through setter method injection
This subject is taught by Nilang
```

To enable `<context:annotation-config />` in Spring XML configuration files, you need to include a few schema definitions specific to context, such as `xmlns:context`, and add `context-specific xsd` into `schemaLocation`.

Now everything works as expected. Objects of the `professor` bean are injected into objects of the `subject` bean properly. This is what we want to achieve with annotation. But wait a minute. We just removed one element (`<property>`) and added the new one—`<context:annotation-config />`.

Ideally, annotation-based configuration should replace XML-based configuration completely. In previous cases, we are still defining the `<bean>` definition in XML-based configuration. If you remove it, Spring will not create any bean, and will not perform any action for annotation you defined for those beans. This is because `<context:annotation-config />` only works for the `<bean>`s that are defined in Spring's application context (XML) file. So, if there is no `<bean>` defined, there is no meaning of annotation, even though you defined it.

Defining a Java class as <bean> with annotation

The solution to this <indexentry content="annotation-based DI:Java class, defining as with annotation">problem is to define `<context:component-scan>` in an application context (XML) file. When Spring reads this element, it will start scanning the beans from the Java package defined by its attribute, `base-package`. You can instruct Spring to treat the Java class as `<bean>` by declaring class-level annotation `@Component`. In short, defining annotation-based configuration is a two-step process, as follows:

1. **Scanning the package**: This can be done by reading the `base-package` attribute of `<context:component-scan>`. Spring will start scanning for the classes in that Java package.
2. **Defining beans**: Out of Java classes in the said Java package, Spring will consider as `<bean>` only those which have class-level annotation—`@Component` is defined. Let's change our example to incorporate this configuration:

```
//Updated Spring application context (XML) file
<?xml version="1.0" encoding="UTF-8"?>
<beans xmlns="http://www.springframework.org/schema/beans"
    xmlns:xsi="http://www.w3.org/2001/XMLSchema-instance"
    xmlns:context="http://www.springframework.org/schema/context"
    xsi:schemaLocation="http://www.springframework.org/schema/beans
        http://www.springframework.org/schema/beans/spring-beans.xsd
```

```
        http://www.springframework.org/schema/context
        http://www.springframework.org/schema/context/spring-context.xsd">
    <context:annotation-config />
    <context:component-scan base-
package="com.packet.spring.annotation.di"/>
</beans>


//Updated Professor class
@Component
public class Professor {
  @Value(value="Nilang")
  private String name;
  //Constructor
  public Professor() {
    System.out.println("Object of Professor is created");
  }
  public String getName() {
    return name;
  }
  public void setName(String name) {
    this.name = name;
  }
}

//Updated Subject class
@Component
public class Subject {
  private Professor professor;
  public Subject() {
    System.out.println("Object of Subject is created");
  }
  //Setter injection method
  @Autowired
  public void setProfessor(Professor professor) {
    System.out.println("setting the professor through setter method
injection ");
    this.professor = professor;
  }
  public void taughtBy() {
    if(professor !=null) {
      System.out.println("This subject is taught by "+professor.getName());
    }
  }
}
```

Spring will consider `Professor` and `Subject` classes as a `<bean>` through `@Component` annotation, so there is no need to define them in an application context (XML) file. You can inject the value for primitive properties with the `@Value` annotation. In the preceding example, we have set the value of the `name` property of the `Professor` bean with the `@Value` annotation directly at property level. Alternatively, you can inject the primitive values to `property` at a setter method level, as per the following snippet:

```
@Autowired
public void setName(@Value("Komal") String name) {
  this.name = name;
}
```

You need to set the `@Autowired` annotation on the setter method and inject the value of that property with the `@Value` annotation. When you run this code, you will get the desired output, similar to what we got with pure XML-based configuration.

The element `<context:component-scan>` does all the things that `<context:annotation-config />` can. If you keep both of them in application context (XML) files, there is no harm; but then `<context:component-scan>` is just suffice, and you can omit `<context:annotation-config />`.

You can pass multiple packages to `<context:component-scan>` as comma separated string to its `base-package` attribute. What's more, you can define various filters (include and exclude) on `<context:component-scan>` to scan specific subpackages and eliminate others.

 Configuration can be done through annotation or with XML, or by mixing both of them. The DI configured with XML is executed after annotation-based DI. So it's possible that XML-based configuration overrides the annotation-based configuration for a bean's property (setter) wiring.

So far, we have learned about `@Autowired`, `@Component`, and `@Value` annotations. We will see a few more annotations that are used frequently in DI as follows:

Annotation—`@Required`: The `@Required` annotation can be applied to a bean's setter method. It indicates that Spring must populate the value of a property from the setter method either through autowire or explicit setting of a property value. In other words, the bean property must be populated at configuration time. If this is not fulfilled, the container throws an exception.

As an alternative, you can use the @Autowired annotation with the attribute required—@Autowired(required=false). When you set it to false, Spring will ignore this property for autowire if the suitable bean is not available.

Annotation—@Qualifier: By default, the @Autowired annotation works with the type of bean's class. When there is more than one bean with the same type (class) configured, Spring will show an error when you try to autowire it with a property. In this case, you need to use the @Qualifier annotation. It will help to wire the specific bean out of available beans of the same type. You need to specify @Qualifier along with @Autowired to remove the confusion by declaring an exact bean. Let's understand this by looking at the following example:

```
public class Professor {
  private String name;
  //Constructor
  public Professor() {
    System.out.println("Object of Professor is created");
  }
  public String getName() {
    return name;
  }
  public void setName(String name) {
    this.name = name;
  }
}

@Component
public class Subject {
  private Professor professor;
  public Subject() {
    System.out.println("Object of Subject is created");
  }
  //Setter injection method
  @Autowired
  @Qualifier("professor1")
  public void setProfessor(Professor professor) {
    System.out.println("setting the professor through setter method
injection ");
    this.professor = professor;
  }
  public void taughtBy() {
    if(professor !=null) {
      System.out.println("This subject is taught by "+professor.getName());
    }
  }
}
```

```
//Updated Application context (XML) file.

<context:component-scan base-package="com.packet.spring.annotation.di"/>
<bean id="professor1" class="com.packet.spring.annotation.di.Professor">
     <property name="name" value="Ramesh" />
</bean>
<bean id="professor2" class="com.packet.spring.annotation.di.Professor">
     <property name="name" value="Nilang" />
</bean>
```

In the previous code, the `@Qualifier` annotation is added along with `@Autowired`, with the value `professor1` in the `Subject` class. This indicates to Spring to autowire the `professor` bean with `id = professor1`. In the Spring configuration file, we have defined two beans of the `Professor` type with different ID values. In absence of the `@Qualifier` annotation, Spring throws an error. The previous code produces output like the following:

```
...
org.springframework.beans.factory.xml.XmlBeanDefinitionReader
loadBeanDefinitions
INFO: Loading XML bean definitions from class path resource [application-
context.xml]
Object of Professor is created
Object of Subject is created
Object of Professor is created
setting the professor through setter method injection
Object of Professor is created
This subject is taught by Ramesh
```

Now Spring will inject the object of a <indexentry content="annotation-based DI:Java class, defining as with annotation">bean with similar ID as the value of the `@Qualifier` annotation. In previous cases, the object of bean with `id = professor1` is injected into `Subject`.

You might be surprised that we have used XML-based configuration here. It's quite possible to define this with annotation in a Java class, but it's advisable to use XML configuration in case you need to define multiple beans of the same type with different ID.

Annotation with the factory method

We have seen how the `factory` method is created and configured to generate beans with XML-based configuration. Spring supports annotation for the `factory` method also. Let's take the same example, and understand how to write annotation for the `factory` method:

```java
public class Employee {
  private String type;
  public Employee(String type) {
    this.type = type;
  }
  public void showType() {
    System.out.println("Type is :"+type);
  }
}

public class Developer extends Employee {
  public Developer(String type) {
    super(type);
  }
}

public class Manager extends Employee {
  public Manager(String type) {
    super(type);
  }
}

@Component
public class EmployeeService {
  //Instance Factory method with annotation
  @Bean("developerBean")
  public Employee getEmployee(@Value("developer")String type) {
    Employee employee = null;
    if("developer".equalsIgnoreCase(type)) {
      employee = new Developer("developer");
    }else if("manager".equalsIgnoreCase(type)) {
      employee = new Manager("manager");
    }
    System.out.println("Employee of type "+type+" is created");
    return employee;
  }
}

@Component
public class SalaryService {
  private Employee employee;
```

```
@Autowired
public void setEmployee(@Qualifier("developerBean")Employee employee) {
  this.employee = employee;
}
public void showEmployeeType() {
  if(this.employee !=null) {
    this.employee.showType();
  }
}
}

public class DIWithAnnotationFactoryCheck {
  public static void main(String[] args) {
    ApplicationContext springContext = new
ClassPathXmlApplicationContext("application-context.xml");
    SalaryService salaryService =
(SalaryService)springContext.getBean("salaryService");
    salaryService.showEmployeeType();
  }
}
```

`Employee` is a base class having `type` as property. `Developer` and `Manager` extend `Employee`, and set the `type` property in a respective constructor. `EmployeeService` and `SalaryService` are defined as component classes with the `@Component` annotation. Spring will treat both of them as `<bean>`.

`EmployeeService` works as a factory bean, which has a `getEmployee` method. This method has an `@Bean` annotation. The `@Bean` annotation indicates a `factory` method. In this method, we are injecting a primitive value: `developer` to `type` parameter, with the `@Value` annotation. This method generates the object of either `Developer` or `Manager` based on the `type` parameter.

In the preceding code, we are supplying a `developerBean` value to the `@Bean` annotation. This instructs Spring to create a `<bean>` with `id` =developerBean, and a class as `Employee`—a return type from the `getEmployee` (factory) method. In short, the `factory` method in the previous code is equivalent to the following XML configuration:

```
<bean id="employeeService"
class="com.packet.spring.annotation.factory.di.EmployeeService">
</bean>
<bean id="developerBean" factory-method="getEmployee" factory-
bean="employeeService">
    <constructor-arg value="developer"></constructor-arg>
</bean>
```

We have another component class: `SalaryService` . It has a `setEmployee` method, taking the object of `Employee` as a parameter. We have given a qualifier as `developerBean` to the parameter of this method. Since this method is declared as autowired, Spring will inject the object of type `Employee` with `id=developerBean`, which is generated by the `factory` method in `EmployeeService`. So, conclusively, the whole preceding Java code is equivalent to the following XML configuration:

```xml
<bean id="employeeService"
class="com.packet.spring.annotation.factory.di.EmployeeService">
</bean>
<bean id="developerBean" factory-method="getEmployee" factory-
bean="employeeService">
    <constructor-arg value="developer"></constructor-arg>
</bean>

<bean id="salaryService"
class="com.packet.spring.annotation.factory.di.SalaryService">
    <property name="employee" ref="developerBean"/>
</bean>
```

DI with Java configuration

So far, we have seen how to define the configuration with XML and annotation. Spring also supports defining configuration completely in Java classes, and there is no more XML required. You need to provide Java classes that take the ownership of creating the beans. In short, it's a source of bean definition.

A class annotated by `@Configuration` would be considered as Java config for a Spring IoC container. This class should declare methods that actually configure and instantiate the objects of beans that would be managed by containers. All such methods should be annotated with `@Bean`. Spring will consider all such `@Bean` annotated methods as a source of bean. Such methods are kinds of `factory` methods. Let's understand this by looking at the following simple example:

```java
@Configuration
public class JavaBaseSpringConfig {
  @Bean(name="professor")
  public Professor getProfessor() {
    return new Professor();
  }
  @Bean(name="subjectBean")
  public Subject getSubject() {
    return new Subject();
```

```
    }
  }
```

In this code, `JavaBaseSpringConfig` is a configuration class. The `name` attribute in the `@Bean` annotation is equivalent to the `id` attribute of the `<bean>` element. This configuration is equivalent to the following XML configuration:

```
<beans>
    <bean id="professor"
class="com.packet.spring.javaconfig.di.Professor"/>
    <bean id="subjectBean"
class="com.packet.spring.javaconfig.di.Subject"/>
</beans>
```

Once you define all your beans in a configuration class, it can be loaded with application context by a container. Spring provides a separate application context called `AnnotationConfigApplicationContext` to load configuration classes and manage bean objects. It can be used as follows:

```
public class DIWithJavaConfigCheck {
  public static void main(String[] args) {
    ApplicationContext springContext = new
AnnotationConfigApplicationContext(JavaBaseSpringConfig.class);
    Professor professor = (Professor)springContext.getBean("professor");
    Subject subject = (Subject)springContext.getBean("subjectBean");
  }
}
```

You need to pass a configuration class in the constructor of `AnnotationConfigApplicationContext`, and the rest of the process of getting beans is identical to other application contexts. Also, there is no change in the way beans are wired with Java config. For example, in the previous code, objects of type `Professor` can be injected into objects of `Subject`, as per the following snippet:

```
public class Professor {
  private String name;
  //Constructor
  public Professor() {
    System.out.println("Object of Professor is created");
  }
  public String getName() {
    return this.name;
  }
  @Autowired
  public void setName(@Value("Komal") String name) {
    this.name = name;
```

```
    }
  }

  public class Subject {
    private Professor professor;
    public Subject() {
      System.out.println("Object of Subject is created");
    }
    //Setter injection method
    @Autowired
    public void setProfessor(Professor professor) {
      System.out.println("setting the professor through setter method
  injection ");
      this.professor = professor;
    }
    public void taughtBy() {
      if(professor !=null) {
        System.out.println("This subject is taught by "+professor.getName());
      }
    }
  }
```

You can notice in the preceding code that we haven't put a @Component annotation for
the Professor and Subject class. This is because the logic of instance creation is within
the methods of the configuration class, so there is no need to ask Spring to scan the Java
package explicitly.

Spring still provides support scanning of specific Java package to create the bean, instead of
creating it yourself with a new operator. For this, you need to apply the following changes:

```
@Configuration
@ComponentScan(basePackages="com.packet.spring.javaconfig.di")
public class JavaBaseSpringConfig {
}

@Component("professor")
public class Professor {
  private String name;
  //Constructor
  public Professor() {
    System.out.println("Object of Professor is created");
  }
  public String getName() {
    return this.name;
  }
  @Autowired
  public void setName(@Value("Komal") String name) {
```

```
    this.name = name;
  }
}

@Component("subjectBean")
public class Subject {
  private Professor professor;
  public Subject() {
    System.out.println("Object of Subject is created");
  }
  //Setter injection method
  @Autowired
  public void setProfessor(Professor professor) {
    System.out.println("setting the professor through setter method
injection ");
    this.professor = professor;
  }
  public void taughtBy() {
    if(professor !=null) {
      System.out.println("This subject is taught by "+professor.getName());
    }
  }
}
```

In the previous code snippet, we declared the `Professor` and `Subject` classes as components by declaring the `@Component` annotation. We also instructed the configuration class—`JavaBaseSpringConfig`, to scan the specific Java package with annotation `@ComponentScan`, and pass the Java package value in the `basePackage` attribute. In both of the previous cases, you will get identical output. This is equivalent to the following XML configuration:

```xml
<?xml version="1.0" encoding="UTF-8"?>
<beans xmlns="http://www.springframework.org/schema/beans"
xmlns:xsi="http://www.w3.org/2001/XMLSchema-instance"
    xmlns:context="http://www.springframework.org/schema/context"
xsi:schemaLocation="http://www.springframework.org/schema/beans
      http://www.springframework.org/schema/beans/spring-beans.xsd
      http://www.springframework.org/schema/context
      http://www.springframework.org/schema/context/spring-context.xsd">

    <bean id="professor" class="com.packet.spring.javaconfig.di.Professor">
        <property name="name" value="komal" />
    </bean>
    <bean id="subjectBean" class="com.packet.spring.javaconfig.di.Subject"
autowire="byType">
    </bean>
</beans>
```

In conclusion, the following diagram shows how a Spring IoC container manages the process of object creation and dependency management:

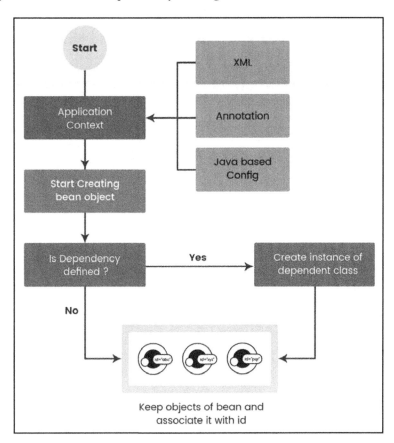

Summary

In this chapter, we learned how you can implement DI with Spring—one of the most popular frameworks for developing enterprise applications today. We have seen how the Spring container plays a vital role for managing bean life cycle.

We also learned how to define configurations that are XML and annotation-based. We also looked at different types of DI in depth, such as setter-based injection and constructor-based injection.

If you want to write your custom logic while creating instances of beans, you can now use the `factory` method in Spring. We also learned how to bind beans automatically with various modes, such as autowire by name, type, and constructor.

With the help of Java config, you can build Spring applications with zero XML. We saw various techniques for using Java config in the last section.

We will continue our journey and learn how to achieve DI in Google Guice, another popular framework that provides containers to achieve loosely coupled systems. We will explore them in the next chapter.

Dependency Injection with Google Guice

4

Since our journey began, we have learned the concepts of the DI pattern to understand IoC, got an idea about the modular framework of Java 9 and its DI mechanism, and in the last chapter, we acquired knowledge of the most widely used Spring Framework to understand DI using various examples.

In this chapter, we will see the rudiments of the **Google Guice** framework and its DI mechanism, and we will also learn various injection types and binding techniques while defining DI in Guice.

A brief introduction to the Google Guice framework

We learned the benefits of DI in software engineering, but choosing a framework wisely is also important when implementing DI because each framework has its own advantages and disadvantages. There are various Java-based dependency injection frameworks available in the open source community, such as Dagger, Google Guice, Spring DI, JAVA EE 8 DI, and PicoContainer.

Here, we will learn in detail about Google Guice (pronounced *juice*), a lightweight DI framework that helps developers to modularize applications. Guice encapsulates annotation and generics features introduced by Java 5 to make code type-safe. It enables objects to wire together and tests with fewer efforts. Annotations help you to write error-prone and reusable code.

In Guice, the `new` keyword is replaced with `@inject` for injecting dependency. It allows constructors, fields, and methods (any method with multiple numbers of arguments) level injections. Using Guice, we can define custom scopes and circular dependency, and it has features to integrate with Spring and AOP interception.

Moreover, Guice also implements **Java Specification Request (JSR) 330**, and uses the standard annotation provided by JSR-330. The first version of Guice was introduced by Google in 2007 and the latest version is Guice 4.1.

Guice setup

To make our coding simple, throughout this chapter, we are going to use a Maven project to understand Guice DI. Let's create a simple Maven project using the following parameters: `groupid:`, `com.packt.guice.id`, `artifactId : chapter4`, and `version : 0.0.1-SNAPSHOT`. By adding `Guice 4.1.0` dependency on the `pom.xml` file, our final `pom.xml` will look like this:

```
<project xmlns="http://maven.apache.org/POM/4.0.0"
xmlns:xsi="http://www.w3.org/2001/XMLSchema-instance"
  xsi:schemaLocation="http://maven.apache.org/POM/4.0.0
http://maven.apache.org/maven-v4_0_0.xsd">
  <modelVersion>4.0.0</modelVersion>
  <groupId>com.packt.guice.di</groupId>
  <artifactId>chapter4</artifactId>
  <packaging>jar</packaging>
  <version>0.0.1-SNAPSHOT</version>
  <name>chapter4</name>
  <dependencies>
    <dependency>
      <groupId>junit</groupId>
      <artifactId>junit</artifactId>
      <version>4.12</version>
      <scope>test</scope>
    </dependency>
    <dependency>
      <groupId>com.google.inject</groupId>
      <artifactId>guice</artifactId>
      <version>4.1.0</version>
    </dependency>
  </dependencies>
  <build>
    <finalName>chapter2</finalName>
  </build>
</project>
```

For this chapter, we have used JDK 9, but not as a module project because the Guice library is not available as a Java 9 modular jar.

Dependency injection and JSR-330

Before diving into Guice injection, let's look at the DI pattern again, along with JSR-330, in brief.

A dependency injection mechanism enables an object to pass dependencies to another object. In Java, using DI, we can move dependency resolution from compile time to runtime. DI removes hard dependency between two Java classes; this allows us to reuse class as much as and also classes are independently testable.

Java Specification Request-330: There is a different way to define dependency in Java classes, but @Inject and @Named are the most common annotations used to describe dependencies in Java classes from JSR-330. According to JSR-330, objects can be injected into the class constructor, the parameter of the method, and a field level. As per best practices, static field and method-level injection should be avoided for the following reasons:

- Static field only injected when the first-time class object was created via DI, which makes static field inaccessible for the constructor
- At runtime, the compiler complains if a static field is marked as final
- When the first instance of the class is created, only static methods are called

As per JSR-330, the injection can be performed in this order: first, constructor injection; then field injection; and the last is method level injection. But, you can't expect the methods or fields to be called in the sequence of their assertion in the class.

 A constructor can't use injected member variables, because field and method parameter injection takes place only after calling a constructor.

Example of simple DI

`NotifictionService` represents a common service interface for sending data to a different system:

```
public interface NotificationService {
    boolean sendNotification(String message, String recipient);
}
```

The previous interface defines a method signature for `sendNotification()` by passing the message and recipient details and returning the type as Boolean. `SMSService.java` is a concrete implementation of this interface for sending SMS notifications:

```
public class SMSService implements NotificationService {

  public boolean sendNotification(String message, String recipient) {
    // Code for sending SMS
    System.out.println("SMS message has been sent to " + recipient);
    return true;
  }
}
```

The previous class implemented code for sending SMS by accepting the message and recipient details. Now, we create a client application, `NotificationClient.java`, which will use `NotificationService` to initialize the actual SMSService. The same object can be used to send notifications to different systems, including email or custom notifications:

```
public class NotificationClient {

  public static void main(String[] args) {
    NotificationService notificationService = new SMSService();
    notificationService.sendNotification("Hello", "1234567890");
  }

}
```

In the previous example, even though implementation and interface are loosely coupled, we need to create a manual instance of the real implementation of the class in the client application. In this scenario, at compilation time, the client application knows which execution classes related to interfaces will be bound.

That is the thing that Google Guice does; it takes instances as services from the client application code and the dependency between the clients, and their service is consequently injected through a simple configuration mechanism.

Let's see an example of dependency injection in Guice by using different API in the next topic.

Basic injection in Guice

We have seen a basic DI implementation, now it is time to understand how injection works in Guice. Let's rewrite the example of a notification system using Guice, and along with that, we will see several indispensable interfaces and classes in Guice. We have a base interface called NotificationService, which is expecting a message and recipient details as arguments:

```
public interface NotificationService {
   boolean sendNotification(String message, String recipient);
}
```

The SMSService concrete class is an implementation of the NotificationService interface. Here, we will apply the @Singleton annotation to the implementation class. When you consider that service objects will be made through injector classes, this annotation is furnished to allow them to understand that the service class ought to be a singleton object. Because of JSR-330 support in Guice, annotation, either from javax.inject or the com.google.inject package, can be used:

```
import javax.inject.Singleton;
import com.packt.guice.di.service.NotificationService;

@Singleton
public class SMSService implements NotificationService {

   public boolean sendNotification(String message, String recipient) {
      // Write code for sending SMS
      System.out.println("SMS has been sent to " + recipient);
      return true;
   }

}
```

In the same way, we can also implement another service, such as sending notifications to a social media platform, by implementing the NotificationService interface.

It's time to define the consumer class, where we can initialize the service class for the application. In Guice, the `@Inject` annotation will be used to define `setter-based` as well as `constructor-based` dependency injection. An instance of this class is utilized to send notifications by means of the accessible correspondence services. Our `AppConsumer` class defines `setter-based` injection as follows:

```
import javax.inject.Inject;

import com.packt.guice.di.service.NotificationService;


public class AppConsumer {

  private NotificationService notificationService;

  //Setter based DI
  @Inject
  public void setService(NotificationService service) {
    this.notificationService = service;
  }
  public boolean sendNotification(String message, String recipient){
    //Business logic
    return notificationService.sendNotification(message, recipient);
  }
}
```

Guice needs to recognize which service implementation to apply, so we should configure it with the aid of extending the `AbstractModule` class, and offer an implementation for the `configure()` method. Here is an example of an injector configuration:

```
import com.google.inject.AbstractModule;
import com.packt.guice.di.impl.SMSService;
import com.packt.guice.di.service.NotificationService;


public class ApplicationModule extends AbstractModule{

  @Override
  protected void configure() {
    //bind service to implementation class
    bind(NotificationService.class).to(SMSService.class);
  }

}
```

In the previous class, the module implementation determines that an instance of
SMSService is to be injected any place a NotificationService variable is determined. In
the same way, we just need to define a binding for the new service implementation, if
required. Binding in Guice is similar to wiring in Spring:

```
import com.google.inject.Guice;
import com.google.inject.Injector;
import com.packt.guice.di.consumer.AppConsumer;
import com.packt.guice.di.injector.ApplicationModule;

public class NotificationClient {

  public static void main(String[] args) {

    Injector injector = Guice.createInjector(new ApplicationModule());

    AppConsumer app = injector.getInstance(AppConsumer.class);

    app.sendNotification("Hello", "9999999999");
  }
}
```

In the previous program, the Injector object is created using the Guice
class's createInjector() method, by passing the ApplicationModule class's
implementation object. By using the injector's getInstance() method, we can initialize the
AppConsumer class. At the same time as creating the AppConsumer's objects, Guice injects
the needy service class implementation (SMSService, in our case). The following is the
yield of running the previous code:

SMS has been sent to Recipient :: 9999999999 with Message :: Hello

So, this is how Guice dependency injection works compared to other DI. Guice has
embraced a code-first technique for dependency injection,
and management of numerous XML is not required.

Let's test our client application by writing a **JUnit** test case. We can simply mock the service
implementation of SMSService, so there is no need to implement the actual service.
The MockSMSService class looks like this:

```
import com.packt.guice.di.service.NotificationService;

public class MockSMSService implements NotificationService {

  public boolean sendNotification(String message, String recipient) {
    System.out.println("In Test Service :: " + message + "Recipient :: " +
```

```
recipient);
    return true;
  }

}
```

The following is the JUnit 4 test case for the client application:

```
import org.junit.After;
import org.junit.Assert;
import org.junit.Before;
import org.junit.Test;

import com.google.inject.AbstractModule;
import com.google.inject.Guice;
import com.google.inject.Injector;
import com.packt.guice.di.consumer.AppConsumer;
import com.packt.guice.di.impl.MockSMSService;
import com.packt.guice.di.service.NotificationService;

public class NotificationClientTest {
    private Injector injector;
    @Before
    public void setUp() throws Exception {
      injector = Guice.createInjector(new AbstractModule() {
        @Override
        protected void configure() {
          bind(NotificationService.class).to(MockSMSService.class);
        }
      });
    }
    @After
    public void tearDown() throws Exception {
      injector = null;
    }
    @Test
    public void test() {
      AppConsumer appTest = injector.getInstance(AppConsumer.class);
      Assert.assertEquals(true, appTest.sendNotification("Hello There",
"9898989898"));;
    }
}
```

Take note that we are binding the `MockSMSService` class to `NotificationService` by having an anonymous class implementation of `AbstractModule`. This is done in the `setUp()` method, which runs for some time before the test methods run.

Guice API and Phases

We have seen DI examples using various Guice APIs, including interfaces and classes. So, it is time to understand the principal API and architecture. Guice architecture is divided into two phases: Start-up and runtime.

Start up phase

In the start-up phase, APIs such as `Module`, `AbstractModule`, `Binder`, `Injector`, `Guice`, and `Provider` play a significant role in Guice dependency injection. Let us learn about each API in detail, starting with **module interface**.

Module interface

This is a special interface that you use to tell Guice which implementations go with which interfaces. Modules are objects that preserve a set of **bindings**. It is viable to have multiple modules in a piece of software. Injectors interact with modules to get the feasible bindings.

The module is represented by using an interface with a method referred to as `Module.configure()`, which ought to be overridden with the aid of the application to populate the bindings. If we rewrite our `ApplicationModule` by implementing the `Module` interface, then it would look like this:

```
import com.google.inject.Module;
import com.packt.guice.di.impl.SMSService;
import com.packt.guice.di.service.NotificationService;

public class ApplicationModule implements Module{

  @Override
  protected void configure(Binder binder) {
    //bind NotificationService to SMSService implementation class
    //Guice will create a single instance of SMSService for every Injection
    binder.bind(NotificationService.class).to(SMSService.class);
  }
}
```

The AbstractModule class

To improve things, there is an abstract class called `AbstractModule`, which straightforwardly extends the module interface, so applications can rely upon `AbstractModule` as opposed to module.

It's strongly suggested that modules should be extended to the usage of `AbstractModule`. It gives a more readable configuration, and additionally steers us away from the excessive invoking of methods on the binder.

In our example `ApplicationModule`, to configure Guice instead of implementing the module interface, we have used `AbstractModule`, where Guice passes our module to the binder interface.

 In the event that an application has a predetermined number of configurations, they could be consolidated in a solitary module. For such applications, a single module per package or a single module per application could be a suitable system.

Binder

This interface mainly includes information associated with **bindings**. A binding normally consists of a mapping between an interface and a concrete implementation. For example, if we consider an implementation of the module interface for creating custom module, then the reference to the interface `NotificationService` is bound to the `SMSService` implementation.

When coding, notice that the objects for both the interface and implementation classes are passed to the `bind()` and then `to()` methods:

```
binder.bind(NotificationService.class).to(SMSService.class);
```

The second way is to tie an interface directly to its instance by writing the following code:

```
binder.bind(NotificationService.class).to(new SMSService());
```

Injector

An `Injector` interface creates and maintains object graphs, tracks dependencies of each type, and uses bindings to inject them. Injectors keep a set of **default bindings**, from which they take configuration details for making and maintaining relationships between objects. Consider the following code, which will return an implementation of the `AppConsumer` class:

```
AppConsumer app = injector.getInstance(AppConsumer.class);
```

We can also get all the associated bindings with the injector by calling
the `Injector.getBindings()` method, which returns a map containing binding objects:

```
Map<Key, Binding> bindings = injector.getBindings()
```

From this, we can say that each binding has a matching `key` object, which is internally made
and kept by the Google Guice class.

Guice

`Guice` is a final class, an entry point to the Guice framework. It's used to create injectors by
providing a set of modules:

```
//From NotificationClient.java
Injector injector = Guice.createInjector(new ApplicationModule());

//Syntax from actual Guice Class
Injector injector = Guice.createInjector(
                new ModuleA(),
                new ModuleB(),
                . . .
                new ModuleN(args)
);
```

In the preceding code snippet, notice that the `createInjector()` method takes
`ApplicationModule()` as an argument; the same method also takes a `varargs`, which
means we can pass zero or more modules separated by a comma.

Provider

By default, whenever an application requires an instance of an object, Guice instantiates and
returns it; but, in some cases, if the object creation process needs customization, then Guice
providers do that. A provider interface takes after the conventional factory design in
making objects. For instance, consider our `ApplicationModule` class binding process:

```
binder.bind(NotificationService.class).to(new SMSProvider());
```

By writing above line of code, `SMSProvider` class gives factory methods that will return objects of type `NotificationService`. Let's say we want to customize the object-making and maintenance process for the `ServiceConnection` class, which is shown as follows:

```
public class ServiceConnection {

    public void startService(){
        System.out.println("Start SMS Notification Service");
    }

    public void stopService(){
        System.out.println("Stop SMS Notification Service");
    }

}
```

Now let's compose a straightforward `Provider` interface that acclimates to Guice `Provider` that makes and returns `ServiceConnection` objects. The following is the code for this:

```
import com.google.inject.Provider;

public class SMSProvider implements Provider{

    @Override
    public ServiceConnection get() {

        // Write some custom logic here.
        ServiceConnection serviceConnection = new ServiceConnection();
        // Write some custom logic here.
        return serviceConnection;
    }
}
```

Every custom provider class should implement `Provider` interface, and must override the `get()` method to get back the objects made in a custom mold. Presently, the module should be aware about the custom provider class so that Guice asks `SMSProvider` to create instances, instead of making them on its own. The following is a module snippet that contains the test client code:

```
import javax.inject.Provider;

import com.google.inject.Binder;
import com.google.inject.Guice;
import com.google.inject.Injector;
import com.google.inject.Module;

public class NotificationClientTest {

    public static void main(String args[]){
        Injector injector = Guice.createInjector(
            new Module(){
                @Override
                public void configure(Binder binder) {
binder.bind(ServiceConnection.class).toProvider((Class<? extends Provider<?
extends ServiceConnection>>) SMSProvider.class);
                }
            }
        );

        ServiceConnection serviceConnection =
        injector.getInstance(ServiceConnection.class);
        serviceConnection.startService();
        serviceConnection.stopService();
    }
}
```

We have seen the use of major API individually, which has a notable role in Guice's start-up phase. The following is the sequence diagram of our application, which illustrates the complete flow of Guice dependency management:

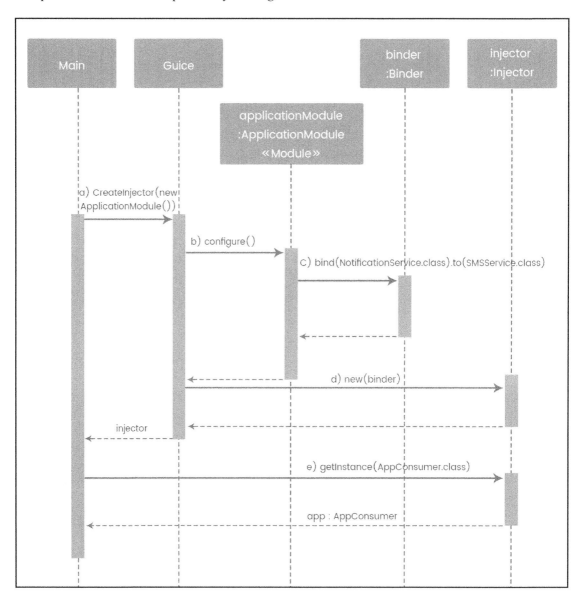

Runtime phase

We will now be able to utilize the injector we made during the start-up phase to inject objects and examine our bindings. Guice's runtime phase consists of an injector which contains a few bindings:

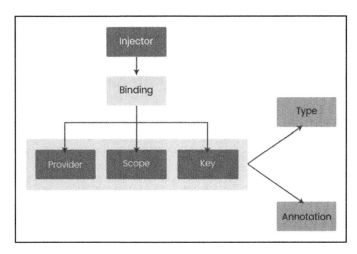

The preceding diagram defines the components of each binding. Each **key** uniquely recognizes each binding. The key consists of a type, which the client depends on, and an annotation, which is optional. An **annotation** could be used to distinguish a couple of bindings of the same type.

Every single binding has a provider, which gives an instance of the mandatory type. We may offer a class, and Guice will make instances of it for us. We might give Guice an instance of the type for binding the class. Guice can inject dependencies if we provide our own **provider**.

By default, no bindings have a scope; but it's optionally available, and for each injection, Guice creates a new instance, which is similar to Spring **Prototype.** Guice also provides a facility to define a custom scope to govern whether or not Guice makes a new instance. In this case, we can make one instance per HttpSession.

Guice annotations

Guice comes with a little set of valuable annotations that are utilized to include metadata values in an application. Now, let's study the annotations that are going to get secured in this segment.

Inject

Guice provides the `@Inject` annotation to indicate that a consumer is dependent on a particular dependency. The injector takes care of initializing this dependency using the object graph. Guice gets a hint from the annotation that it needs to participate in the class construction phase. The `@Inject` annotation can be utilized in a constructor for a class, for a method, or for a field. Consider the following code:

```
//Field level injection
@Inject
private NotificationService notificationService;

//Constructor level Injection
@Inject
public AppConsumer(NotificationService service){
    this.notificationService=service;
}

//Method  level injection
@Inject
public void setService(NotificationService service) {
    this.notificationService = service;
}
```

ProvidedBy

If we need to customize the object creation process for a few interface types, at that point we would depend on the Guice Provider component. Let's say, for the `NotificationService` interface, we need `SMSProvider` to make and return objects of type `SMSService`. In such a case, we can authorize the provider type for the interface by specifically explaining it in the interface statement. Consider the following code snippet, `NotificationService.java`;

```
@ProvidedBy(SMSProvider.class)
public interface NotificationService{

}
//@ProvidedBy is equivalent to toProvider() binding like below,
bind(NotificationService.class).toProvider(SMSProvider.class)
```

ImplementedBy

This annotation focuses on a class object that gives an implementation to the interface. For example, in case the `NotificationService` interface has numerous usages, and in case we wish to have `SMSService` as the default implementation, at that point we can code as follows:

```
@ImplementedBy(SMSService.class)
public interface NotificationService{
    boolean sendNotification(String message, String recipient);
}
```

@Named

Making unused annotation types for each concrete usage doesn't provide much value, as the sole reason for having such an annotation is to check the implementation class instance required by clients. To support such things, we have a built-in binding annotation called `@Named`, which takes a string. There's the method `Names.named()`, which returns `@Named` annotation when passing names as arguments:

```
bind(NotificationService.class).annotatedWith(Names.named("SMS"))
        .to(SMSService.class);
```

We suggest utilizing `@Named` sparingly, because the compiler cannot check the string.

`@Singleton` is another useful annotation which we will discuss in detail in `Chapter 5`, *Scopes*.

Binding in Guice

In the previous topic, we became acquainted with the binding process and its importance in Guice DI. Each binding call to the `bind()` method is type-checked, so the compiler can report mistakes in case you utilize off-base types.

Guice provides different types of binding techniques which can be used in modules. The types of binding available are: linked bindings, instance bindings; untargeted bindings. Constructor bindings, built-in bindings, Just-in-time bindings. and provider bindings.

Linked bindings

Linked binding helps to map a type to its implementation. Examples of linked bindings include an interface to its implementation class, and a superclass to a subclass.

Here, NotificationService is bound to the SMSService instance in the ApplicationModule class. This binding affirmation binds an interface to its implementation:

```
bind(NotificationService.class).to(SMSService.class);
```

When we call injector.getInstance(ApplicationModule.class), it will utilize SMSService. If binding to a distinctive implementation of NotificationService, as an EmailService is required, then we only need to essentially alter the binding:

```
bind(NotificationService.class).to(EmailService.class);
```

We can even define the link from a type to any of its subtypes, such as an executing class or an extending class. You can indeed link the concrete SMSService course to a subclass:

```
bind(SMSService.class).to(SMSDatabase.class);
```

A basic thing to be understood is that linked binding could indeed be chained. For example, if we need SMSService to be wired to a specific class which extends the SMSService, at that point we would do something like this:

```
public class ApplicationModule implements AbstractModule{
  @Override
  protected void configure() {
    //Linked binding as chain
    bind(NotificationService.class).to(SMSService.class);
    bind(SMSService.class).to(SMSDataBase.class);
  }

}
```

Here, if asked for NotificationService, then the injector will return the SMSDataBase instance.

Instance bindings

Instance bindings help to bind a type to a particular instance of that type. This is normally helpful only for objects that don't have dependencies in their possession; for example, value objects:

```
Public class SearchModule extends AbstractModule{
    @Override
    protected void configure() {
        bind(SearchParameters.class).toInstance(new SearchParameters());
    }
}
```

Avoid utilizing `.toInstance` with objects that are complicated to make, since it can slow down application start-up. You can utilize the `@Provides` technique.

Untargeted bindings

Binding that can be created without target is known as an untargeted bindings. These are really signs to the injector around a type, so that the dependencies are arranged eagerly. In **untargeted binding**, we do not require the `to` clause:

```
bind(SampleConcreteClass.class).in(Singleton.class);
//Another way to define untargeted binding
bind(String.class).toInstance("./alerts/");
```

In this statement, the injector would prepare an instance of the String class eagerly with a value of `./alerts/`. When dependency injection requires it to inject the instance of String, it will inject this specific instance. This binding is useful when defining concrete classes and types annotated by `@ImplementedBy` or `@ProvidedBy`.

Constructor bindings

This kind of binding binds a type to a constructor. This specific case arises when the `@Inject` annotation can't be implemented to the target constructor. Possible reasons for this could be:

- If we are using a third-party class
- A couple of constructors taking part in dependency injection

To address such a problem, we have the `toConstructor()` binding in our module. Here, if the constructor cannot be found, module reflectively select our target constructor and handle the exception:

```
public class SampleModule extends AbstractModule {
  @Override
  protected void configure() {
    try {
      bind(NotificationService.class).toConstructor(
          SMSService.class.getConstructor(SMSDatabaseConnection.class));
    } catch (NoSuchMethodException e) {
      e.getPrintStackTrace();
    }
  }
}
```

In the previous code, `SMSService` should have a constructor that takes a single `SMSDatabaseConnection` parameter. Guice will conjure that constructor to fulfill the binding, so the constructor does not require an `@Inject` annotation. If we select reflective constructor then we require to handle checked exceptions thrown by the `getConstructor()` API.

The scope of each constructor binding is autonomous. In the event that we make different singleton bindings that target the same constructor, every binding yields its possess instance.

Built-in bindings

As the name suggests, these are bindings that are automatically covered in the injector. Let the injector make these bindings, as trying to bind them yourself is an error. **Loggers** is one example of this.

- **Loggers**: `java.util.logging.Logger` has a built-in binding in Guice. The binding naturally sets the logger's title to the title of the class into which the logger is being injected:

```
@Singleton
public class SMSDatabaseLog implements DatabaseLog {

  private final Logger logger;

  @Inject
```

```
public SMSDatabaseLog(Logger logger) {
   this.logger = logger;
}

public void loggerException(UnreachableException e) {
   //Below message will be logged to the SMSDatabaseLog by logger.
   logger.warning("SMS Database connection exception, " + e.getMessage());
}
```

Just-in-time Bindings

These are bindings that might be made by Guice automatically. When there is not a clear binding, the injector will endeavor to make a binding, which is a **Just-in-time (JIT)** binding or implicit binding.

Default constructors: By default, no argument constructors are invoked to get instances ready for injection. Occasionally, in our illustrations there is no express binding as a way to make an instance of Client. In any case, the injector invoked a default constructor to return the instance of the client.

Constructors with @Inject: If constructors have the @Inject annotation, then that moreover qualified for implicit bindings. It also includes no arguments and a public constructor:

```
//Constructor Based Injector
@Inject
public AppConsumer(NotificationService notificationService){
    this.service = notificationService;
}
```

Binding annotations

Sometimes we want to use numerous bindings for the same type. In our earlier example, NotificationService is bound to SMSService, which is essentially futile since the interface is bound to just one execution. If we need the client to have the adaptability to utilize any of the implementations, at that point we need to write a couple of bind statements in the configure() method, and to make that possible, we can write code as follows:

```
bind(NotificationService.class).annotatedWith("sms").to(SMSService.class);
bind(NotificationService.class).annotatedWith("email").to(EmailService.class
);
```

From the previous statement, Guice knows when to bind the `NotificationService` interface to `SMSService` and when to bind it to `EmailService`.

The client-side code to call the `SMSService` implementation will look like this:

```
AppConsumer app = injector.getInstance(@Named("sms") AppConsumer.class);
```

And to call `EmailService` implementation:

```
AppConsumer app = injector.getInstance(@Named("email") AppConsumer.class);
```

To support such a case, binding supports non-mandatory *binding annotations*. A **key** is a pair of unique combinations of Annotation and Type. The following is the basic code to define binding annotations for SMS annotation:

```
@BindingAnnotation @Target({ FIELD, PARAMETER, METHOD })
@Retention(RUNTIME)
public @interface SMS{}
```

From the previous two lines, let's look at the meta-annotations:

- `@BindingAnnotation` is utilized to tell Guice that this is a binding's explanation. If we ever define a different binding for the same member, then Guice may produce an error.
- `@Target` and `@Retention` are typical annotations used to create custom annotations in Java. `@Target`, helps to locate field, parameter, and method, and `@Ratention(RUNTIME)` available in runtime respectively.

Guice injection

As we know what dependency injection is, let us explore how Google Guice provides injection.

We have seen that the injector helps to resolve dependencies by reading configurations from modules, which are called *bindings*. *Injector* is preparing charts for the requested objects.

Dependency injection is managed by injectors using various types of injection:

- Constructor injection
- Method injection
- Field injection
- Optional injection
- Static injection

Constructor Injection

Constructor injection can be achieved by using the `@Inject` annotation at the constructor level. This constructor ought to acknowledge class dependencies as arguments. Multiple constructors will, at that point, assign the arguments to their final fields:

```java
public class AppConsumer {

    private NotificationService notificationService;

    //Constructor level Injection
    @Inject
    public AppConsumer(NotificationService service){
        this.notificationService=service;
    }
    public boolean sendNotification(String message, String recipient){
      //Business logic
      return notificationService.sendNotification(message, recipient);
    }
}
```

If our class does not have a constructor with `@Inject`, then it will be considered a default constructor with no arguments. When we have a single constructor and the class accepts its dependency, at that time the constructor injection works perfectly and is helpful for unit testing. It is also easy because Java is maintaining the constructor invocation, so you don't have to stress about objects arriving in an uninitialized state.

Method injection

Guice allows us to define injection at the method level by annotating methods with the `@Inject` annotation. This is similar to the setter injection available in Spring. In this approach, dependencies are passed as parameters, and are resolved by the injector before invocation of the method. The name of the method and the number of parameters does not affect the method injection:

```
private NotificationService notificationService;
//Setter Injection
@Inject
public void setService(NotificationService service) {
    this.notificationService = service;
}
```

This could be valuable when we don't want to control instantiation of classes. We can, moreover, utilize it in case you have a super class that needs a few dependencies. (This is difficult to achieve in a constructor injection.)

Field injection

Fields can be injected by the `@Inject` annotation in Guice. This is a simple and short injection, but makes the field untestable if used with the `private` access modifier. It is advisable to avoid the following:

```
@Inject private NotificationService notificationService;
```

Optional injection

Guice provides a way to declare an injection as optional. The method and field might be optional, which causes Guice to quietly overlook them when the dependencies aren't accessible. **Optional injection** can be used by mentioning the `@Inject(optional=true)` annotation:

```
public class AppConsumer {
  private static final String DEFAULT_MSG = "Hello";
  private string message = DEFAULT_MSG;
  @Inject(optional=true)
  public void setDefaultMessage(@Named("SMS") String message) {
    this.message = message;
  }
}
```

Static injection

Static injection is helpful when we have to migrate a static factory implementation into Guice. It makes it feasible for objects to mostly take part in dependency injection by picking up access to injected types without being injected themselves. In a module, to indicate classes to be injected on injector creation, use `requestStaticInjection()`. For example, `NotificationUtil` is a utility class that provides a static method, `timeZoneFormat`, to a string in a given format, and returns the date and timezone. The `TimeZoneFormat` string is hardcoded in `NotificationUtil`, and we will attempt to inject this utility class statically.

Consider that we have one private static string variable, `timeZonFmt`, with setter and getter methods. We will use `@Inject` for the setter injection, using the `@Named` parameter.

`NotificationUtil` will look like this:

```
@Inject static String timezonFmt = "yyyy-MM-dd'T'HH:mm:ss";

@Inject
public static void setTimeZoneFmt(@Named("timeZoneFmt")String timeZoneFmt){
 NotificationUtil.timeZoneFormat = timeZoneFmt;
 }
```

Now, `SMSUtilModule` should look like this:

```
class SMSUtilModule extends AbstractModule{
    @Override
    protected void configure() {
        bindConstant().annotatedWith(Names.named(timeZoneFmt)).to(yyyy-MM-
dd'T'HH:mm:ss);
        requestStaticInjection(NotificationUtil.class);
    }
}
```

 This API is not suggested for common utilization, since it faces many of the same issues as static factories. It is also difficult to test and it makes dependencies uncertain.

Summary

So, that's it for Google Guice. To sum up our chapter, we began with basic dependency injection. After that, we learned how basic Dependency Injection works in Guice, with examples.

Then, we investigated the phases of Guice, and the role of the API in each phase. We got the idea that, unlike Spring, in Guice there is no requirement to maintain isolated XML files, as all the setup-related data is nicely typified by means of the module component.

In the middle of the chapter, we explored the major annotations and distinct types of binding available in Guice, and at the end, we learned the different types of injections.

In the next chapter, we will become competent in the different scopes offered by Spring and the Google Guice framework.

5
Scopes

On this journey, we've learned dependency injection concepts in Java 9, Spring, and Google Guice, with the help of examples.

In `Chapter 3`, *Dependency Injection with Spring*, and `Chapter 4`, *Dependency Injection with Google Guice,* we came across the word scope, which is a very important element of Spring beans and Google Guice. So, let's understand what a scope is, and why it is important when talking about dependency injection.

In this chapter, we will first learn about various scopes provided by Spring, and how they can be defined for Spring beans. We will also learn the relation between bean scope and dependency injection. Finally, we will look into the scopes available in Google Guice. The topics we are going to cover are as follows:

- Introduction to bean scopes in Spring
- How to define a bean scope
- Dependency injection and bean scopes
- How to choose a bean scope
- Scopes in Google Guice

Introduction to bean scopes in Spring

In `Chapter 3`, *Dependency Injection with Google Guice,* we learned about different Spring modules along with dependency injection. In Spring, beans are the backbone of an application, and they are managed by a Spring IOC container. A bean is a class or object that is created using the configuration of metadata that we can pass to an IOC container. Before learning about scope, let's define a bean in Spring.

Bean definition

The metadata of a **bean** has its own properties with independent bean definitions. Some of these bean definitions are as follows:

- **Class**: This will be used to create a bean, and it is mandatory to mention a class name for which we are supposed to create a bean.
- **Name**: If we want to define different aliases for the bean, then we use the name attribute, with the help of a separator, such as a comma (,) or semicolon (;). When we have XML-based configuration, we can use the name and/or id attribute as an identifier for a bean. A bean with an id attribute is preferred, because it is mapped with an actual XML ID element.
- **Constructor-arg**: A constructor argument is used to inject dependencies by passing a parameter as an argument in a constructor, which we saw in Chapter 3, *Dependency Injection with Spring*.
- **Properties**: We can directly pass properties with key-value pairs in a Spring bean for injecting. This is useful sometimes if we need to pass certain fixed values to a bean.
- **Autowiring mode**: Autowiring can be used to reduce the use of properties and constructor arguments. To enable autowiring mode, we need to use the autowire attribute in a Spring bean. Attributes can have values such as byName, byType, and constructor.
- **Lazy initialization mode**: By default, a Spring bean is created with a singleton scope, which initializes all the properties in eager mode. If a bean is defined with lazy mode, then an IOC container creates a bean instance the first time the request comes, rather than during the startup process.
- **Initialization method**: Spring initialization works after all the properties are set by an IOC container. In XML-based configuration, we can define an init method by defining an init-method attribute. The init method should be void, and without arguments. A @PostConstruct annotation can be used for initializing methods.
- **Destruction method**: On completion of a bean lifecycle, if we have to close resources or want to perform actions before destruction of a bean, we can use the destroy-method attribute of a bean in XML configuration.
  The @PreDestroy annotation is also used instead of the XML attribute.

The following configuration file contains different types of bean definition syntax and for that, the `application-context.xml` file could be:

```xml
<?xml version="1.0" encoding="UTF-8"?>
<beans xmlns="http://www.springframework.org/schema/beans"
    xmlns:xsi="http://www.w3.org/2001/XMLSchema-instance"
    xsi:schemaLocation="http://www.springframework.org/schema/beans
        http://www.springframework.org/schema/beans/spring-beans.xsd">

    <!-- A simple bean definition with ID and Class Name-->
    <bean id = "..." class = "...">
        <!-- Bean configuration and properties like constructor-arg -->
    </bean>
    <!-- Bean definition using Name attribute instead of ID attribute -->
    <bean name = "..." class = "...">
        <!-- Bean configuration and properties like constructor-arg -->
    </bean>
    <!-- Ban definition with constructor arguments -->
    <bean id="..." class="...">
        <constructor-arg ref="..."/>
        <constructor-arg ref="..."/>
    </bean>
    <!-- Ban definition for autowiring using byName mode -->
    <bean id="..." class="..." autowire="byName">
    <!-- Bean configuration and properties like constructor-arg -->
    </bean>
    <!-- Ban definition for defining scope -->
    <bean id="..." class="..." scope="prototype">
    <!-- Bean configuration and properties like constructor-arg -->
    </bean>
    <!-- Ban definition with lazy initialization mode -->
    <bean id = "..." class = "..." lazy-init = "true">
        <!-- Bean configuration and properties like constructor-arg -->
    </bean>

    <!-- Bean definition which has initialization method -->
    <bean id = "..." class = "..." init-method = "init">
        <!-- Bean configuration and properties like constructor-arg -->
    </bean>

    <!-- Bean definition which has destruction method -->
    <bean id = "..." class = "..." destroy-method = "destroy">
        <!-- Bean configuration and properties like constructor-arg -->
    </bean>
</beans>
```

Lazy instantiation is most effective when the scope is **singleton**. With the **prototype** scope, a bean initializes with lazy mode by default.

Spring scopes

We have understood how a bean definition works with different attributes, and **scope** is one of the attributes in a bean definition. Before going on to learn about scope types, one question comes to mind: what are scopes?

If we look from a Spring perspective, the meaning of **scope** is, *to characterize the life cycle of a bean and define visibility of that bean within a specific context in which the bean is utilized.* When the scope of the object ends, it will be considered **out of scope** and can no longer be injected into different instances.

 From the **The Oxford English Dictionary**, scope means "*the extent of the area or subject matter that something deals with or to which it is relevant.*"

Spring has seven scopes, and out of them, five are used for web application development. The following is a diagram of **Bean Scopes**:

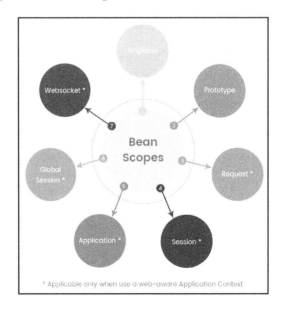

Singleton scope

Each bean created by a Spring container has a default **Singleton** scope; Spring treats it as one instance of the bean, and it is served for each request for that bean from the cache inside the container. In dependency injection, a bean defined as a singleton is injected as a shared bean from the cache.

A **Singleton** bean scope is restricted to the Spring container, compared to this Singleton pattern in Java, where only one instance of a specific class will ever be created per `ClassLoader`. This scope is useful in web applications as well as standalone applications, and stateless beans can also utilize a **Singleton** scope.

On the off chance that three beans have distinctive IDs but the same class with a **Singleton** scope, at that point, three instances will be made of that class and in terms of bean ID, as only one instance of the singleton bean is made:

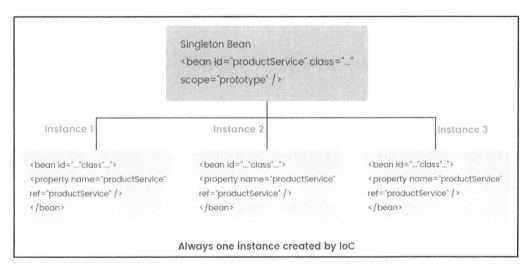

Prototype scope

When we need to create multiple instances of a bean, then we use the **prototype** scope. A `prototype` scoped bean is mostly used for stateful beans. So, on each and every request, a new instance of the bean will be created by the IoC container. This bean can be injected into another bean, or used by calling a `getBean()` method of a container.

But, a container does not maintain the record of a `prototype` bean after initialization. We have to implement a custom `BeanPostProcessor` to release the resources occupied by the **prototype** bean. A `destroy` method of the life cycle is not called in the case of a **prototype** scope, only initial `call-back` methods are called for all the objects irrespective of scope:

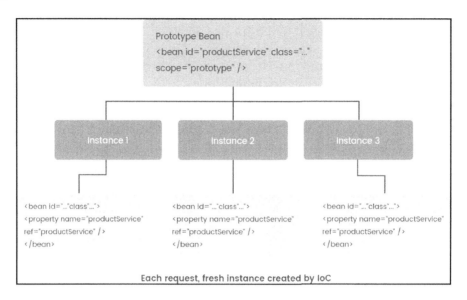

So far, we have seen **Singleton** and **Prototype** scopes. Both can be used in standalone and web applications, but there are five more scopes that only work in web applications. If we used these scopes with `ClassPathXmlApplicationContext`, then it will throw an `IllegalStateException` for an unknown scope.

To use the **request**, **session**, **global session**, **application**, and **websocket** scopes, we need to use a web-aware application context implementation (`XmlWebApplicationContext`). Let's look at all the web scopes in detail.

Request scope

In a web application, every HTTP request from a client gets a new bean instance if the bean is scoped as a **request**. On an HTTP request completion, a bean will immediately be considered out of scope, and memory will be released. If a server has 100 concurrent requests, then there will be 100 distinct instances of a bean class available. If there is any change in one instance, it will not affect other instances. Following is an image of the request scope:

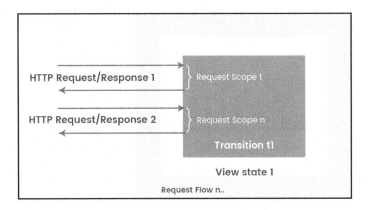

Session scope

A **session** is a group of interactive information, also known as a *conversion* between client and server within a specific time frame on a website. In an **Apache Tomcat** server, the default time frame of one session is 30 minutes, which includes all the operations made by a user.

The Spring session bean scope is similar to an HTTP session; an IoC container creates a new instance of a bean for each user session. On user logout, its session bean will be out of scope. Like a request, if 50 users are concurrently using a website, then a server has 50 active sessions, and a Spring container also has 50 different instances of a bean class:

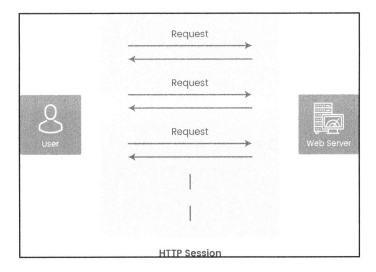

The previous image illustrates that all HTTP requests from the user are included in a single session, and all requests may have lifetime access of a single bean instance in that session scope. Session instances are destroyed, as before long, the session is destroyed/quit on the server.

Application scope

The application scope only works on a web application. An IoC container creates single instances of bean definitions per web application during runtime. Following are two ways to define the application scope:

```
// 1) XML way to configure define application scope
<bean id="..." class="com.packt.scope.applicationBeanTest"
scope="application" />

// 2) Java config using annotation
@Component
@Scope("application")
public class applicationBeanTest {
}

//or

@Component
@ApplicationScope
public class applicationBeanTest {
}
```

This is the same as the Singleton scope, but the main difference is that a Singleton scope bean is worked as a Singleton per `ApplicationContext`, whereas an application scope bean is worked as Singleton per `ServletContext`. These beans are stored as attributes in `ServletContext`.

Global session scope

A **global session scope** is similar to a session scope. The only difference is that it will be used in a Portlet application. Global sessions can be used when we have an application that is built on the JSR-168, JSR-286, and JSR-362 portal specifications. There will be multiple sites/applications that work under a single portlet container.

Portlet containers have different portlets, and all have their own portlet context, as well as portlet session. Portlet sessions work with the portlet boundary, but when we have to share common information between multiple sites, then we can define beans with a `globalSession` scope. Spring has separate portlet MVC modules for portal applications:

```
// 1) XML way to configure define application scope
<bean id="..." class="com.packt.scope.globalBeanTest" scope="globalSession"
/>

// 2) Java config using annotation
@Component
@Scope("globalSession")
public class globalBeanTest {
}

//or

@Component
@GlobalSessionScope
public class globalBeanTest {
}
```

Consider an intranet application that consists of server sites. Users could be members of multiple sites. In such scenarios, user preferences with common information can be stored as global sessions for the logged-in user, and the same will be utilized between multiple sites and portlets. The following image shows how **Global Sessions** are shared between portlet containers:

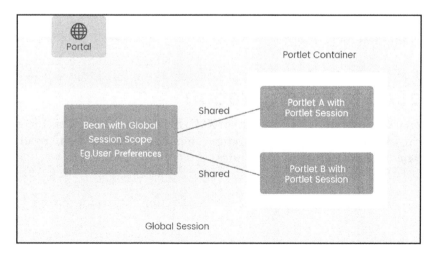

websocket scope

This scope is used when two-way communication between a customer and remote site is enabled using the **websocket** protocol. It is mainly useful when applications are used by multiple users with simultaneous actions.

Here, an HTTP request is used to do an initial handshake, and once it is established, the TCP port remains open for a client and server for communication. The websocket bean is similar to a singleton, and injected into Spring controllers. The life of a websocket bean is longer compared to a typical websocket session. The following example shows how a websocket is declared using Scope annotation and traditional XML configuration:

```
//Using @Scope annotation
@Scope(scopeName = "websocket")

//Using XML configuration
<bean id="..." class="com.packt.scope.WebsocketExampleTest"
scope="websocket" />
```

How to define a bean scope

So, we understand the different scopes and their usage. Now it is time to see how we can use them in coding. We will mainly look at singleton and prototype bean scopes with examples.

Spring provides two different ways to write an application: one is traditional XML metadata configuration, and the second is Java configuration using annotations. Let's look at how XML configuration is used.

XML metadata configuration

In Spring, bean configuration is declared in an XML file of our choice. This file is used by an IoC container to initialize the application context, and at the same time, all bean definitions are initialized based on the provided attribute.

Using the singleton scope

The singleton scope is a very common scope used in major applications. Here, we will start to use the singleton scope. First, we will create a bean class named `EmailService`, which consists of a simple `getter/setter` method and `Constructor` method with a `print` statement:

```
package com.packt.springbean;

public class EmailService {
  private String emailContent;
  private String toAddress;
  public EmailService() {
    System.out.print(" \n Object of EmailService is Created !!! ");
  }
  public String getEmailContent() {
    return emailContent;
  }
  public void setEmailContent(String emailContent) {
    this.emailContent = emailContent;
  }
  public String getToAddress() {
    return toAddress;
  }
  public void setToAddress(String toAddress) {
    this.toAddress = toAddress;
  }
}
```

Every Spring application requires a context file that describes the configuration of the beans. Configuration of the previously mentioned bean class can be written as follows in `application-context.xml`:

```
<?xml version="1.0" encoding="UTF-8"?>
<beans xmlns="http://www.springframework.org/schema/beans"
  xmlns:xsi="http://www.w3.org/2001/XMLSchema-instance"
  xsi:schemaLocation="http://www.springframework.org/schema/beans
        http://www.springframework.org/schema/beans/spring-beans.xsd">

  <bean id="emailService" class="com.packt.springbean.EmailService"
    scope="singleton" />
</beans>
```

Here, in the bean definition, we have mentioned `emailService` as an ID attribute, and a class name provided as `com.packt.springbean.EmailService` to point our bean class to the package path. For learning purposes, we have used a `scope` attribute with a `singleton` value.

If the `scope` attribute is not defined in the bean definition, then by default, a Spring IoC container creates an instance of the bean with a singleton scope. Now, let's check what will happen if we try to access the `EmailService` bean two times. For that, let's use the `SpringBeanApplication.java` class:

```
//SpringBeanApplication.java

package com.packt.springbean;

import org.springframework.context.ApplicationContext;
import org.springframework.context.support.ClassPathXmlApplicationContext;

public class SpringBeanApplication {

  public static void main(String[] args) {
    ApplicationContext context = new ClassPathXmlApplicationContext(new
String[] { "application-context.xml" });
    // Retrieve emailService bean first time.
    EmailService emailServiceInstanceA = (EmailService)
context.getBean("emailService");
    emailServiceInstanceA.setEmailContent("Hello, How are you?");
    emailServiceInstanceA.setToAddress("krunalpatel1410@yahoo.com");
    System.out.println("\n Email Content : " +
emailServiceInstanceA.getEmailContent() + " sent to "+
emailServiceInstanceA.getToAddress() );

    // Retrieve emailService bean second time.
    EmailService emailServiceInstanceB = (EmailService)
context.getBean("emailService");
    System.out.println("\n Email Content : " +
emailServiceInstanceB.getEmailContent() + " sent to "+
emailServiceInstanceB.getToAddress() );

  }
}
```

In a standalone application, the Spring context is acquired using `ClassPathXMLApplicationContext` by passing a context file as a parameter in a String array. A Spring IoC container initializes the application context, and returns an object of it.

A bean is retrieved by passing a bean `name` in the form of an argument in the `getBean()` method. In the preceding example, we get two instances of the `EmailService` bean using the `getBean()` method. But, the first time we are only setting the value into a bean and we are getting the same by writing `printing message`. Even a constructor creates an object of bean only once.

So, when we run `SpringBeanApplication`, the output would be as follows:

```
Feb 09, 2018 6:45:15 AM
org.springframework.context.support.AbstractApplicationContext
prepareRefresh
INFO: Refreshing
org.springframework.context.support.ClassPathXmlApplicationContext@6fc6f14e
: startup date [Fri Feb 09 06:45:15 IST 2018]; root of context hierarchy
Feb 09, 2018 6:45:15 AM
org.springframework.beans.factory.xml.XmlBeanDefinitionReader
loadBeanDefinitions
INFO: Loading XML bean definitions from class path resource [application-
context.xml]

 Object of EmailService is Created !!!
 Email Content : Hello, How are you? sent to krunalpatel1410@yahoo.com

 Email Content : Hello, How are you? sent to krunalpatel1410@yahoo.com
```

Since the `EmailService` bean has the Singleton scope, the second instance of `emailServiceInstanceB` prints the message with a value set by `emailServiceInstanceA` as well, even though it is `get` by a new `getBean()` method. The Spring IoC container creates and maintains only a single instance of a bean per container; no matter how many times you reclaim it with `getBean()`, it will continuously return the same instance.

Using the prototype scope

As we have seen, the **prototype scope** is used to get a new instance of a bean every time when requested. To understand prototype, we will take the same bean class, `EmailService`, and we just need to change the value of the scope attribute for the `emailService` bean in `application-context.xml`:

```
<?xml version="1.0" encoding="UTF-8"?>
<beans xmlns="http://www.springframework.org/schema/beans"
  xmlns:xsi="http://www.w3.org/2001/XMLSchema-instance"
  xsi:schemaLocation="http://www.springframework.org/schema/beans
        http://www.springframework.org/schema/beans/spring-beans.xsd">
```

```
    <bean id="emailService" class="com.packt.springbean.EmailService"
      scope="prototype" />
</beans>
```

The code used for the singleton scope will the same as before, while the output of the preceding code will be as follows:

```
Feb 09, 2018 7:03:20 AM
org.springframework.context.support.AbstractApplicationContext
prepareRefresh
INFO: Refreshing
org.springframework.context.support.ClassPathXmlApplicationContext@6fc6f14e
: startup date [Fri Feb 09 07:03:20 IST 2018]; root of context hierarchy
Feb 09, 2018 7:03:20 AM
org.springframework.beans.factory.xml.XmlBeanDefinitionReader
loadBeanDefinitions
INFO: Loading XML bean definitions from class path resource [application-
context.xml]

  Object of EmailService is Created !!!
  Email Content : Hello, How are you? sent to krunalpatel1410@yahoo.com

  Object of EmailService is Created !!!
  Email Content : null sent to null
```

From output, the EmailService constructor is called two times, and gets a new instance for each getBean() method called. For the second instance, emailServiceInstanceB, we get a null value, because we haven't set any value for that.

Java configuration using annotations

Once annotation was introduced in Java 1.5, Spring Framework also added support for annotations in version 2.5.

Spring provides several standard annotations, which are used on stereotype classes in the application. By using such annotations, we don't need to maintain bean definitions in XML files. We just need to write one line, <context:component-scan>, in the Spring XML configuration for a scanning component, and the Spring IoC container scans the defined package to register all the annotated classes and their bean definitions in the application context.

Specifically, @Component and @Service are used to scan beans in the provided package. Here, we will use @Service annotation, because the @Service annotation is too specialized for the @Component annotation. It doesn't give us any extra behavior than the @Component explanation, but it's better to choose @Service over @Component in service-layer classes, since it indicates expectations way better.

For singleton and prototype beans, our application-context.xml file will be the same, and looks as follows:

```
<?xml version="1.0" encoding="UTF-8"?>
<beans xmlns="http://www.springframework.org/schema/beans"
    xmlns:xsi="http://www.w3.org/2001/XMLSchema-instance"
    xmlns:context="http://www.springframework.org/schema/context"
    xsi:schemaLocation="http://www.springframework.org/schema/beans
        http://www.springframework.org/schema/beans/spring-beans.xsd
        http://www.springframework.org/schema/context
        http://www.springframework.org/schema/context/spring-context.xsd">

    <!-- <context:annotation-config /> -->
    <context:component-scan base-package="com.packt.springbeanannotation" />
</beans>
```

Singleton scope with annotation

@Scopes annotation is used to indicate the scope of a bean, either singleton, prototype, request, session, or a few custom scopes.

To make the EmailService bean class a singleton, we need to annotate the class with @Scope and @Service. So, our EmailService class will look as follows:

```
package com.packt.springbeanannotation;

import org.springframework.context.annotation.Scope;
import org.springframework.stereotype.Service;

@Service
@Scope("singleton")
public class EmailService {
  private String emailContent;
  private String toAddress;
  public EmailService() {
    System.out.print(" \n Object of EmailService is Created !!! ");
  }
  public String getEmailContent() {
    return emailContent;
```

```
    }
    public void setEmailContent(String emailContent) {
      this.emailContent = emailContent;
    }
    public String getToAddress() {
      return toAddress;
    }
    public void setToAddress(String toAddress) {
      this.toAddress = toAddress;
    }
  }
```

We will use the same `SpringBeanApplication.java` class to test our annotation changes, and the output will also be the same as the XML configuration example.

Prototype scope with annotation

To use prototype scope with annotations, we only need to mention `prototype` in the `@Scope` annotation instead of `singleton`. So, our `EmailService.java` class will be the same, except we change the annotation value, and it will look as follows:

```
@Service
@Scope("prototype")
public class EmailService {
    ...
}
```

As like the XML example output, this will also create a new instance each time it is called. In a similar way, we can use other scopes, such as request, session, application, and global session, using XML metadata or annotations.

Dependency injection and the bean scope

We understand each scope has a different boundary. Now, we will write one REST controller to understand how different scope beans are injected to other reference beans by writing simple Spring boot applications.

In the following diagram, the **StudentController** has injected the reference to all other classes. The `ClassDetail` class with the `session` scope has two references to singleton and prototype, and the student application contains a few other associations between classes as well. **Autowired** annotation is utilized to fulfill dependency between beans. Just to clarify, Spring controllers are always created with the singleton scope:

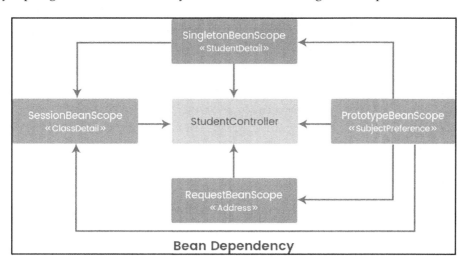

As we are writing a Spring boot application with REST. Will will have to create a maven project and the configuration of `pom.xml` file would be:

```xml
<?xml version="1.0" encoding="UTF-8"?>
<project xmlns="http://maven.apache.org/POM/4.0.0"
xmlns:xsi="http://www.w3.org/2001/XMLSchema-instance"
    xsi:schemaLocation="http://maven.apache.org/POM/4.0.0
http://maven.apache.org/xsd/maven-4.0.0.xsd">
    <modelVersion>4.0.0</modelVersion>

    <groupId>com.packt.java9.beanscope</groupId>
    <artifactId>spring-beanscope-test</artifactId>
    <version>0.1.0</version>

    <parent>
        <groupId>org.springframework.boot</groupId>
        <artifactId>spring-boot-starter-parent</artifactId>
        <version>1.5.8.RELEASE</version>
    </parent>

    <dependencies>
        <dependency>
```

```
            <groupId>org.springframework.boot</groupId>
            <artifactId>spring-boot-starter-web</artifactId>
        </dependency>
    </dependencies>

    <properties>
        <java.version>9</java.version>
    </properties>

    <build>
        <plugins>
            <plugin>
                <groupId>org.springframework.boot</groupId>
                <artifactId>spring-boot-maven-plugin</artifactId>
            </plugin>
        </plugins>
    </build>

</project>
```

We start with the StudentController class, injected with four beans that have different scopes defined:

```
package com.packt.java9.beanscope.controller;

import org.springframework.beans.factory.annotation.Autowired;
import org.springframework.web.bind.annotation.RequestMapping;
import org.springframework.web.bind.annotation.RestController;

import com.packt.java9.beanscope.beans.PrototypeBeanScope;
import com.packt.java9.beanscope.beans.RequestBeanScope;
import com.packt.java9.beanscope.beans.SessionBeanScope;
import com.packt.java9.beanscope.beans.SingletonBeanScope;


@RestController
public class StudentController {

  public StudentController() {
    System.out.println(" ::::::::::::::::::::: StudentController
Initialized ::::::::::::::::: ");
  }

  @Autowired
  PrototypeBeanScope prototypeBeanScope;

  @Autowired
```

```
    SessionBeanScope sessionBeanScope;

    @Autowired
    RequestBeanScope requestBeanScope;

    @Autowired
    SingletonBeanScope singletonBeanScope;

    @RequestMapping("/")
    public String index() {
      sessionBeanScope.printClassDetail();
      requestBeanScope.printAddress();
      return " Greetings from Student Department !!";
    }

}
```

To understand each scope, I have created simple interfaces with scope names for better visualization, and this will also help when we add the dependency of one bean into another bean. @Scope annotation is utilized to mention the StudentDetail bean as a singleton and it is implementing the SingletonBeanScope interface. This class has been injected with a PrototypeBeanScope bean. Moreover, we are printing incremental values of the static integer variable increment to track how many times the singleton bean is initialized in the constructor. The same is written for all other bean classes. StudentDetail.java will be as follows:

```
package com.packt.java9.beanscope.beans;

import org.springframework.beans.factory.annotation.Autowired;
import org.springframework.context.annotation.Scope;
import org.springframework.stereotype.Service;

@Service
@Scope("singleton")
public class StudentDetail implements SingletonBeanScope {

  /* Inject PrototypeBeanScope to observer prototype scope behaviour */
  @Autowired
  PrototypeBeanScope prototypeBeanScope;

  private static int increment = 0;

  /**
   * Every time this bean is initialized, created variable will be
increases by
   * one.
```

```
   */
  public StudentDetail() {
    super();
    System.out.println(" \n :::::::: Object of StudentDetail bean is created
" + (++increment) + " times :::::::: ");
  }
}
```

`SubjectPreference.java` is defined with a prototype bean scope as follows:

```
package com.packt.java9.beanscope.beans;

import org.springframework.context.annotation.Scope;
import org.springframework.stereotype.Component;

@Component
@Scope("prototype")
public class SubjectPreference implements PrototypeBeanScope {

  private static int increment = 0;

  /**
   * Every time this bean is initialized, created variable will be
increases by
   * one.
   */
  public SubjectPreference() {
    System.out.println(" \n :::::::: Object of SubjectPreference with
Prototype scope is created " + (++increment)
        + " Times :::::::: \n ");
  }

}
```

The request scope and session scope are only worked in a web-aware application context. `Address.java` is annotated with the request scope:

```
package com.packt.java9.beanscope.beans;

import org.springframework.beans.factory.annotation.Autowired;
import org.springframework.context.annotation.Scope;
import org.springframework.context.annotation.ScopedProxyMode;
import org.springframework.stereotype.Component;

@Component
@Scope(value = "request", proxyMode = ScopedProxyMode.TARGET_CLASS)
public class Address implements RequestBeanScope {
```

```
private static int increment = 0;

/* Inject PrototypeBeanScope to observer prototype scope behaviour */
@Autowired
PrototypeBeanScope prototypeBeanScope;

/**
 * Every time this bean is initialized, created variable will be
increases by
 * one.
 */
public Address() {
  System.out.println(
      " \n :::::::: Object of Address bean with Request scope created " +
(++increment) + " Times :::::::: ");
}

public void printAddress() {
  System.out.println("\n :::::::::::::::: RequestbeanScope ::
printAddress() Called :::::::::::::::: ");
}
}
```

In the same way, the `session` scope is used in the `ClassDetail.java` class:

```
package com.packt.java9.beanscope.beans;

import org.springframework.beans.factory.annotation.Autowired;
import org.springframework.context.annotation.Scope;
import org.springframework.context.annotation.ScopedProxyMode;
import org.springframework.stereotype.Repository;

@Repository
@Scope(value = "session", proxyMode = ScopedProxyMode.TARGET_CLASS)
public class ClassDetail implements SessionBeanScope {

  /* Inject SingletonBeanScope to observer session scope behaviour */
  @Autowired
  SingletonBeanScope singletonBeanScope;

  /* Inject PrototypeBeanScope to observer prototype scope behaviour */
  @Autowired
  PrototypeBeanScope prototypeBeanScope;

  private static int increment = 0;

  /**
   * Every time this bean is initialized, created variable will be
```

```
increases by
   * one.
   */
  public ClassDetail() {
     System.out.println(" \n :::::::: Object of ClassDetail bean with session
scope created " + (++increment)
        + " Times ::::::: ");
  }

  public void printClassDetail() {
     System.out.println("\n ::::::::: Session Bean - PrintMessage Method
Called ::::::::::::::::::: ");
     System.out.println("\n ::::::::: SessionBeanScope :: printClassDetail()
Called :::::::::::::::: ");
  }
}
```

An extra `proxyMode` attribute is utilized to make an intermediary, which will be injected as a dependency by Spring, and Spring starts the `target` bean when it's required. Note that there is no dynamic request when the web application setting is initialized.

On a successful run, we will see the following console log:

```
2018-02-11 20:16:53.168  INFO 12152 --- [ost-startStop-1] o.s.b.w.servlet.FilterRegistrationBean   : Mapping filter: 'httpPutFormContentFilter' to: [/*]
2018-02-11 20:16:53.168  INFO 12152 --- [ost-startStop-1] o.s.b.w.servlet.FilterRegistrationBean   : Mapping filter: 'requestContextFilter' to: [/*]

::::::: Object of StudentDetail bean is created 1 times :::::::

::::::: Object of SubjectPreference with Prototype scope is created 1 Times  :::::::

::::::::::::::::::::::: StudentController Initialized :::::::::::::::::

::::::: Object of SubjectPreference with Prototype scope is created 2 Times  :::::::
```

Following is the analysis of the output:

- The `StudentDetail` bean is created only once, which is, at most, a singleton class, and it loads during application startup.
- Subsequently, the `SubjectPreference` bean is created with the prototype scope. It is injected into the `StudentDetail` singleton bean and, because of that, it also initializes with it. Here, we all know that the prototype scope bean is created each time it is called.
- Here, the `StudentDetail` singleton bean depends on `PrototypeBeanScope`, which is implemented by the `SubjectPreference` class, and dependencies are resolved at instantiation time. So, the first instance of `SubjectPreference` is created, and then it will be injected into the `StudentDetail` singleton bean.

- The Spring container is initializing the StudentController class only one time because controller is, by default, a singleton.
- As StudentController has injected a reference of the PrototypeBeanScope, once again an instance of the SubjectPreference bean is created. Controllers also have a reference of the SingletonbeanScope bean, but an instance of that is not created again, because it is already loaded.
- An instance of SessionScopeBean and RequestScopeBean is not created, because there is no HTTP request or HTTP session at this instant.

To check the request and session scope, go to http://localhost:8080 in a browser and observe the console log:

```
2018-02-11 20:42:48.484  INFO 12152 --- [nio-8080-exec-2] o.s.web.servlet.DispatcherServlet          : FrameworkServlet 'dispatcherServlet': initialization completed in 35 ms
:::::::: Object of  ClassDetail bean with session scope created 1 Times ::::::::
:::::::: Object of SubjectPreference with Prototype scope is created 3 Times  ::::::::
:::::::::: SessionBeanScope :: printClassDetail() Called :::::::::::::::::
:::::::: Object of Address bean with Request scope created  1 Times  ::::::::
:::::::: Object of SubjectPreference with Prototype scope is created 4 Times  ::::::::

::::::::::::::: RequestbeanScope :: printAddress() Called :::::::::::::::
```

The log shows that one instance each for the ClassDetail and Address classes are created because they define with the session and request scope respectively. Both the ClassDetail and Address classes also injected PrototypeBeanScope, and because of that, the SubjectPreference instance has been created two more times—a total of four times.

Enter http://localhost:8080 URL again:

```
:::::::::: SessionBeanScope :: printClassDetail() Called :::::::::::::::::

:::::::: Object of Address bean with Request scope created  2 Times  ::::::::

:::::::: Object of SubjectPreference with Prototype scope is created 5 Times  ::::::::


::::::::::::::: RequestbeanScope :: printAddress() Called :::::::::::::::
```

It will create one more instance of the Address class, which is marked as a request scope, and a new instance of SubjectPreference class with prototype scope will be created. It will not create an instance of the ClassDetail class because we have not created a new session, our session is still going.

To initiate a new session, we need to close the browser and go to the URL. Open another browser, and go to the URL:

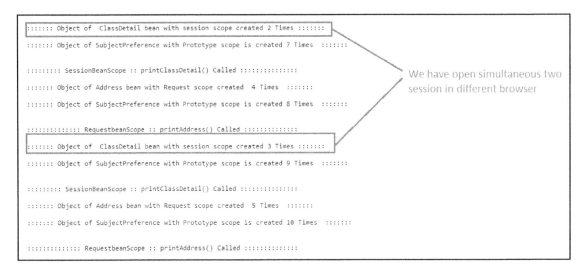

```
::::::: Object of  ClassDetail bean with session scope created 2 Times :::::::
::::::: Object of SubjectPreference with Prototype scope is created 7 Times  :::::::

::::::::: SessionBeanScope :: printClassDetail() Called :::::::::::::::::
::::::: Object of Address bean with Request scope created  4 Times  :::::::
::::::: Object of SubjectPreference with Prototype scope is created 8 Times  :::::::

:::::::::::::: RequestbeanScope :: printAddress() Called :::::::::::::::
::::::: Object of  ClassDetail bean with session scope created 3 Times :::::::
::::::: Object of SubjectPreference with Prototype scope is created 9 Times  :::::::

::::::::: SessionBeanScope :: printClassDetail() Called :::::::::::::::::
::::::: Object of Address bean with Request scope created  5 Times  :::::::
::::::: Object of SubjectPreference with Prototype scope is created 10 Times  :::::::

:::::::::::::: RequestbeanScope :: printAddress() Called :::::::::::::::
```

We have open simultaneous two session in different browser

By doing this, two new sessions will be created, and a total of three instances are created for the `ClassDetail` class, along with two instances of the `Address` class, and two instances of the `SubjectPreference` class.

In the event that we need to inject a request scope bean into another bean of a longer-lived scope, you may select to inject an AOP proxy in the scoped bean. We require to injecting an intermediary object that exposes the same public interface as the scoped object. But that can recover the target object from the applicable scope and provide method calls onto the genuine object.

Furthermore, the bean is going through an intermediate proxy that is serializable. The same bean subsequently can re-obtain the `target` singleton bean by doing deserialization. `<aop:scoped-proxy/>` is used by the beans that are marked as a singleton.

In the same way, when using the prototype bean scope, each method calls on the shared proxy will lead to the creation of a new target instance which the call is, at that point, being sent to.

By default, a CGLIB-based class proxy is made when the Spring holder makes a proxy for a bean that is checked up with the `<aop:scoped-proxy/>` component.

How to choose a bean scope

Each scope in Spring has a different feature, and it falls to us as programmers to know how to utilize those scopes.

In an application, if we have a stateless object and there is no impact on the object creation process then the use of a scope is unnecessary. In contrast, if an object has state then it is advisable to use a scope such as singleton.

When dependency injection is in business, then the singleton scope is not adding much value. In spite of the fact that singletons spare object creation (and afterward garbage collection), synchronization requires us to initialize a singleton bean. Singletons are most valuable for:

- Configuration of stateful beans
- Lookup of objects that are costly to build
- A database association pool object that is associated with resources

If we consider concurrency, classes defined with a singleton or session scope must be thread-safe, and anything injected in these classes should be thread-safe. On the other hand, the request scope cannot be thread-safe.

Scopes in Google Guice

Most of the scopes we have seen for the Spring Framework similarly exist in Google Guice. Scope defines that code should work in a specific context, and in Guice, the Injector manages the scope context. **Default scope** (No Scope), **singleton**, **session**, and **request** are the main scopes in Guice.

Default scope

By default, Guice injects a new and separate instance of an object for each dependency (similar to the prototype scope in Spring), whereas Spring provides singletons by default.

Let us consider an example of a house that has a family with three people, all with their own personal car. Every time they call the `injector.getInstance()` method, a new instance of a car object is available for each family member:

```
home.give("Krunal", injector.getInstance(Car.class));

home.give("Jigna", injector.getInstance(Car.class));

home.give("Dirgh", injector.getInstance(Car.class));
```

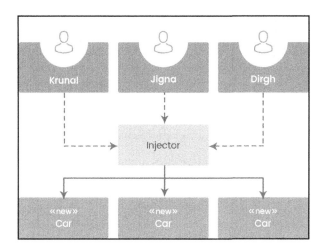

Singleton scope

If we want to create only one instance of the class, then the `@Singleton` annotation can be used to mark the implementation class. As long as a the singleton object lives, the injector lives in context, but in the same application, it is possible to have multiple injectors, and in that case, each injector is associated with a different instance of a singleton-scoped object:

```
@Singleton
public class DatabaseConnection{

    public void connectDatabase(){
    }

    public void disconnectDatabase(){
    }
}
```

Another way to configure a scope is by using a bind statement in the module:

```
public class ApplicationModule extends AbstractModule{

  @Override
  protected void configure() {
    //bind service to implementation class
bind(NotificationService.class).to(SMSService.class).in(Singleton.class);
  }

}
```

When we use linked binding in a module, then the scope only applies to binding the source, not to the `target`. For example, we have a class `UserPref` that implements both `Professor` and `Student` interfaces. This will create two instance of type: one for `Professor` and another one for `Student`:

```
bind(Professor.class).to(UserPref.class).in(Singleton.class);
bind(Student.class).to(UserPref.class).in(Singleton.class);
```

This is because the singleton scope applies at the binding type level, which is `Professor` and `Student`, not at the target type, `UserPref`.

Eager singletons

Guice provides special syntax for making an object that has the singleton scope, and is initialized to eager mode rather than lazy mode. Following is the syntax:

```
bind(NotificationService.class).to(SMSService.class).asEagerSingleton();
```

Eager singletons uncover initialization issues sooner, and guarantee end users get a reliable, smart encounter. Lazy singletons empower a quicker edit-compile-run development cycle. We can utilize the stage enum to indicate which procedure ought to be utilized.

The following table defines stage-wise use of syntax of the singleton and supported object initialize mode:

Syntax	PRODUCTION	DEVELOPMENT
@Singleton	eager*	lazy
.asEagerSingleton()	eager	eager
.in(Singleton.class)	eager	lazy
.in(Scopes.SINGLETON)	eager	lazy

Guice eagerly creates singleton instances only for the modules that are defined as singleton.

`@SessionScoped` and `@RequestedScoped` scope functionality and behavior is the same as Spring in Guice, and it will only be applicable when used in a web application.

Summary

We started the chapter with a Spring bean definition attribute, which is important to learn as the whole IoC container is a relay on bean initialization. After that we learned the classification of scope with syntax.

On our journey, we learned how scope is configured using XML metadata and Java configuration in Spring. Without dependency injection, we cannot complete the chapter. That's why, by writing a **Spring Boot** application, we try to understand how the main scopes work in standalone as well as in web applications.

We intentionally skipped the scope topic in Chapter 4, *Dependency Injection with Google Guice*. So, we have covered the Google Guice scope in this chapter with basic scopes. Spring and Google Guice have almost the same scope, but the default behavior of object initialization is different. Spring creates instances with the singleton, whereas Guice creates with the prototype scope.

In the next chapter, we will look at an important feature called **aspect-oriented programming** in Spring.

6
Aspect-Oriented Programming and Interceptors

So far, we have learned about the concept of dependency injection and its implementation in popular frameworks, such as Spring and Google Guice. We also learned how to control the object creation process by scoping beans based on business requirements. In this chapter, we will learn another way of implementing separation of concerns: **aspect-oriented programming (AOP)**.

AOP solves a different portion of the design problem by isolating repeated code from the application and plugging it in dynamically. AOP, along with **Inversion of Control (IoC)**, brings modularity to the application. AOP helps in organizing your application in layer fashion, which would be impossible in the traditional object-oriented approach.

AOP permits you to intercept the flow of business code and straightforwardly inject a set of functionalities, without touching or altering the original code. This makes your application loosely coupled from those common functionalities. Before we dive into this concept, let's first understand the scenario, what the problem is, and how we can use AOP as an effective solution.

In this chapter, we will discover and discuss the following interesting topics:

- What AOP is, and what problems you can solve with AOP
- How to achieve AOP in Spring Framework
- Choosing AOP frameworks and a style of configuration

AOP introduction

While writing any software application, the best practice is to divide your code into multiple independent modules based on business use cases. For example, you write an **Employee Service** class for all employee-related functions, an **HRService** class for all HR-related functions, and so on and so forth.

In general, the whole application consists of a set of independent classes that span multiple verticals and doesn't share the same class hierarchy. This diagram depicts this scenario:

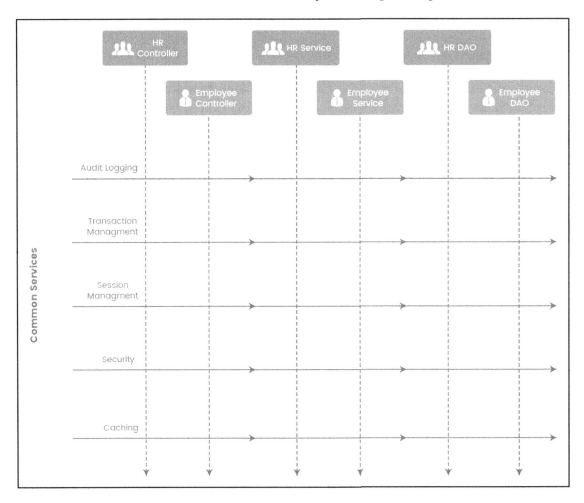

Irrespective of the independent nature of each vertical, there are a few common items you need to implement across all of them, such as **transaction management, session management, audit logging, security, caching,** or any such custom processing mechanism based on rules.

If you wish to implement these common services across verticals with a traditional approach, you need to put them into each of the methods in these classes manually. Taking an example of a logging mechanism, for this, you would need to write a little bit of code at the beginning and end of every method.

This leads to code duplication, as the same logic needs to be placed several times. This leads to a maintenance nightmare in the later part of the application development process when any changes are introduced. Let's understand how.

Suppose, as per your business requirements, you add audit logs after each update and delete method. You put the method name and its time in the log. Now, let's say your business needs to place the name of currently logged-in users in the log. In this case, you need to update the logging details manually in several methods.

This is just one example. You will end up changing the code for each of the common services, spread across multiple verticals. The effective solution is to keep them isolated from verticals. Implement them in one place and plug them into other core business classes as and when required based on certain rules or criteria.

In essence, the core part of the business logic does not have to know that something that is common across multiple classes has been included, removed, or changed, and can keep working as before. Separating common functionalities (cross-cutting concerns in the AOP paradigm) and turning them on and off without touching or modifying the core business logic, will eventually increase modularity and bring great flexibility in terms of maintenance in any application. AOP aims to provide a way to achieve this solution. AOP is mainly used to provide declarative services.

To understand AOP concepts, it's crucial to understand the terminology used in the AOP paradigm:

- **Concern:** This is a behavior or functionality we want to achieve in our application. For example, HR management and employee management are two functionalities, and are thus considered as concerns in AOP.
- **Aspect:** In very simple terms, this is a common behavior that spans multiple classes in the same or different hierarchy. In other words, the common concept that cuts across multiple concerns is called the aspect. In our example, the logging mechanism is called the aspect in AOP terminology.

- **Join-point:** This is a point during the execution flow of the application where you need to apply **Advice**. For example, a method invocation or a place where you need to handle an exception could be join-point.
- **Advice:** This is an action performed on a specific join-point by the AOP framework. Conceptually, it's a common functionality implementation at that join-point. The process of applying **Advice** can be controlled by specifying various types, such as `around`, `before`, `after`, `throws`, and so on.
- **Point-cut:** This is an expression that describes a pattern of applicable join-points. In other words, the AOP framework will apply the **Advice** (common functionality) on join-points (methods) that are described by a point-cut (for example, `set*` means all methods start with the word *set*). We can say a point-cut is a filter criterion to choose join-points in the system.

In most cases, developers get confused between join-point and point-cut. Let's take a real-life example to understand the difference. Suppose you want to buy cooking oil and you go to the department store. You reach the grocery section and find various edible oils made from difference sources, such as sunflower, groundnut, cotton seed, rice brand, corn, and so on.

Your requirement is to choose light oil (in terms of low cholesterol) for your daily needs, and hence you choose either sunflower oil or rice brand oil. In this case, all the available edible oils are the join-points, and your choice of sunflower/rice brand oil, based on your needs, is considered a point-cut. In short, all available options are considered as join-points, while the one you choose, based on your needs, is called a point-cut.

- **Target object:** That is the object in which the common functionalities are being implemented. In other words, this is the object on which the **Advice** is applied by a set of aspects.
- **AOP-Proxy:** Proxy is a design pattern used to encapsulate the object and control access to it. The AOP framework creates a proxy/dynamic object to implement various aspects (in the form of **Advice**). In short, AOP creates a proxy object that looks like the object on which the proxy was created, but with a few additional features. In **Spring Framework**, AOP-proxy is supplied through the JDK or the CGLIB library.
- **Weaving:** As we have seen, the main idea behind AOP is to plug common behaviors (or aspects) into business classes without modifying them. The process of linking such aspects with other classes to apply **Advice** is called weaving.

Weaving can be done at compile or run time. **Spring AOP** supports load-time weaving, while the **AspectJ** framework supports both compile-time and load-time weaving.

- **Compile-time weaving**: In this type of weaving, the process of linking aspects is performed at compile time. The AOP framework will apply the aspects to your Java source file and create a binary class file, which is woven with those aspects. AspectJ uses a special compiler to achieve compile-time weaving.
- **Post-compile-time (or binary) weaving**: This is similar to compile-time weaving. The process of linking aspects is performed on precompiled classes, or JAR files. The aspects that are woven may be in either source or binary form. This, again, can be done through a special compiler. Both compile-time and post-compile-time weaving can be achieved through AspectJ.
- **Runtime weaving**: Compile-time and post-compile-time weaving happens before the actual class file is loaded into memory, whereas runtime (or load-time) weaving happens once the target class is loaded into JVM by the class loader. Runtime weavers are supported by both the Spring AOP and AspectJ frameworks.

The process of weaving can be expressed through the following diagram:

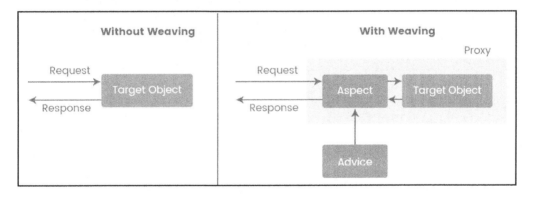

Spring AOP

Spring AOP is purely developed in Java. It doesn't require us to alter or control the class loader hierarchy. Because of this adaptability, you can utilize Spring AOP for a servlet container or application server. At present, Spring AOP only supports applying Advice at method level. In other words, method-level join-points are supported in Spring AOP

Spring supports AOP in conjunction with its IoC capabilities. You can define aspects with normal bean definition, while weaving them with AOP specific configuration. In other words, IoC is used to define aspects, and AOP is used to weave them to other objects. Spring uses both of them to solve common problems. This is how Spring AOP differs from other AOP frameworks.

Spring AOP is a proxy-based framework, and supports runtime weaving of objects. It can be used through either XML-based or AspectJ annotation-based configuration.

XML(schema)-based Spring AOP

Just like a class is the unit of the object-oriented programming paradigm, aspect is the unit of AOP. Modularity is achieved through aspect in an aspect-oriented programming model. If you wish to choose XML-based configuration for AOP, Spring supports defining aspects using `aop` namespace tags. You need to define `aop` namespace tags as follows:

```xml
<?xml version="1.0" encoding="UTF-8"?>
<beans xmlns="http://www.springframework.org/schema/beans"
       xmlns:xsi="http://www.w3.org/2001/XMLSchema-instance"
       xsi:schemaLocation="http://www.springframework.org/schema/beans
       http://www.springframework.org/schema/beans/spring-beans.xsd
       http://www.springframework.org/schema/aop
       http://www.springframework.org/schema/aop/spring-aop.xsd"
       xmlns:aop="http://www.springframework.org/schema/aop">
```

To differentiate AOP-specific configuration, you need to specify all AOP-related artifacts such as aspects, point-cut, Advice, and so on, within an `<aop:config>` element inside your Spring context (XML) file. Multiple `<aop:config>` elements are allowed.

Declaring aspect

The first thing in Spring AOP is to decide on and define the aspects. In XML-based configuration, an aspect is conceptualized as a simple Java class that you need to declare as a bean definition in a Spring application context (XML) file. The `<aop:aspect>` element is used to define an aspect:

```
<aop:config>
<aop:aspect id="myLoggin" ref="loggingAspect"></aop:aspect>
</aop:config>
<bean id="loggingAspect"
class="com.packet.spring.aop.aspects.LogginAspect">
</bean>
```

Since an aspect is a form of Java class, it can be defined as a normal Spring bean, and then can be configured with the `ref` attribute of the `<aop:aspect>` element. The state and behavior is associated with fields and methods of the aspect class, while the point-cut and advice information is configured in the XML. In the previous example, we define logging as an aspect.

After defining an aspect, the next step is to define the join-point through the point-cut. Spring AOP supports method-level join-points only.

In XML schema based-AOP, Spring enables an auto-proxy mechanism with the `<aop:config>` declaration. You do not need to define anything for auto-proxy explicitly; however, if you are enabling auto-proxy with some other mechanism (such as AutoProxyCreator), you should choose either of these options to avoid any runtime issues.

Declaring a point-cut

Just to recall, a join-point is a place where we want to apply **Advice**, and a point-cut represents a pattern of matching join-points. A point-cut must be defined within the `<aop:config>` element. A point-cut can be declared within the `<aop:aspect>` element or outside of it. If it's defined outside of `<aop:aspect>`, it can be shared between multiple aspects and advisors.

A point-cut allows Advice to be applied to the target object independently of the object-oriented hierarchy. Transaction management through AOP Advice in Spring is a real example of where transaction Advice is applied to specific methods (`add`/`update`/`delete` methods) that span multiple object hierarchies. This snippet is one of the possible ways of writing a point-cut:

```
<aop:pointcut id="employeeServiceMethods"
expression="execution(* com.packet.spring.aop.service.*.*(..))" />
```

A point-cut is uniquely identified by its `id` attribute. The `expression` attribute represents the pattern (or filter) of matching join-points. The value of the `expression` attribute consists of two components:

- Point-cut designator
- Pattern

Point-cut designator

A **point-cut designator** (**PCD**) is a keyword (initial word) that tells Spring AOP how to match the point-cut. Spring AOP supports various point-cut designators:

- `execution`: This is used to match method execution (join-points). This is a primary designator, and is used most of the time while working with Spring AOP.
- `within`: This designator has the limitation of matching of join-points within certain types only. It's not as flexible as execution. For example, it's not allowed to specify return types or method parameter mapping. If the patterns with `within` are up to the Java package, it matches all methods of all classes within that package. If the pattern is pointing to a specific class, then this designator will cover all the methods within that class.
- `this`: This restricts the matching of join-points to the beans that are references of a given type in an expression. In other words, the `this` designator is one step narrower than the `within` designator, and expects you to specify a specific class type as a pattern. It will not be allowed to define any wildcard patterns.
- `target`: This limits the matching of join-points, where the target object is an instance of the given type in an expression. The target designator seems similar to the `this` designator, but there is a difference in their use. Let's understand this.

As we have seen, Spring AOP creates proxy objects through either the **JDK** or the **CGLIB** library. Spring AOP uses a JDK-based proxy if the target object implements an interface; otherwise, it selects CGLIB. You should use the `this` designator when CGLIB provides the proxy (that is, your target object doesn't implement an interface), and the target designator when the JDK provides the proxy (the `target` object implements an interface).

- `args`: This designator is generally used for matching method arguments. It allows us to pass wildcards for matching packages, Java classes, return types, or method names.

- `@target`: This PCD filters the join-points where the class of the object has an annotation of a given type. Although the names are equal, the `@target` designator is not similar to the `target` designator. They are different in terms of matching the join-points as follows:

  - The `target` designator: Matches the target object if it is an instance of the given type in an expression

  - The `@target` designator: Matches the target object, if the class of target object has an annotation of given type

- `@within`: This designator restricts matching join-points to within the type that has a given annotation. It allows us to use wildcards to match point-cuts.

- `@annotation`: This PCD is used to match a point-cut of a type that has a given annotation. It's useful to construct point-cuts on classes that have custom annotation.

- `@args`: This designator restricts matching a join-point to where actual runtime objects passed as method arguments have an annotation of a given type. This is useful to narrow down the join-point selection to specific methods from the available overloaded methods in the target class.

Patterns

A pattern is a filter criteria to match possible join-points. It tells Spring AOP what to match. **Patterns** are generally written within brackets, just after the PCD. It's a kind of regular expression in AOP to select the desired join-point.

Spring AOP supports only method-level join-points, and patterns are used to choose specific methods of the target object. A pattern consists of the following expressions in the same order:

- **Access modifier**: For Spring AOP, the only possible value is `public`. This expression is optional.
- **Return type**: This is the fully qualified name of the return type. Putting * for this expression means it allows any return type.
- **Java package**: Java package name can be used.
- **Java class name**: Java class name can be used. Putting * for this expression means it applies to all Java classes under a given package.
- **Method name**: Method name can be given. Putting * in this expression will include all methods of a given class.
- **Method parameters**: Type of parameter can be given. Putting .. (two dots) means any number of parameters for a given method will be considered.
- **Exception details**: Throws a declaration.

The format of a pattern is exactly similar to method signature. Let's understand the meaning of the previous expressions by seeing a few examples.

Example 1 : The following expression will match all public methods of the `EmployeeService` class with the following conditions:

- Method with any return value, including void
- Method with any parameters, including empty parameter method:

Example 2: The following expression will match all public methods with the following conditions:

- Method with any return value, including void
- Method with any parameters, including empty parameter method
- Method of all classes that fall directly under the `com.packet.spring.aop.service` Java package:

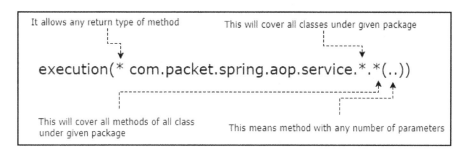

Example 3: The following expression will match all public methods with the following conditions:

- Method with any return value, including void
- Method with any parameters, including empty parameter method
- Method of all classes fall under the `com.packet.spring.aop.service` Java package and its subpackage:

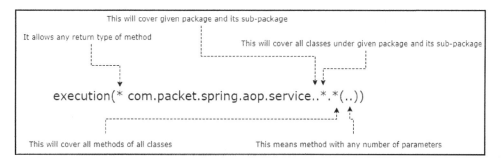

Example 4: The following expression will match all public methods of the EmployeeService class with the following conditions:

- Method with a return type of String only
- Method with any parameters, including an empty parameter method:

Example 5: The following expression will match all public methods of the EmployeeService class with the following conditions:

- Method with any return value, including void
- Method with two parameters, first a String and second a Long, in the same order of method parameter:

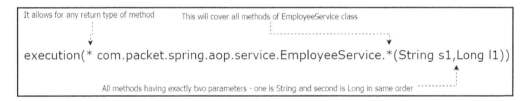

Example 6: The following expression will match all public methods of the EmployeeService class with the following conditions:

- Method with any return value, including void
- Method with one or more parameters, where the first parameter is String only:

Example 7: The following expression will match specific public methods with the following conditions:

- Method name starts with the `find` word
- Method with any return value, including void
- Method with just one parameter of type `String`
- Methods of all classes fall under the `com.packet.spring.aop.service` Java package:

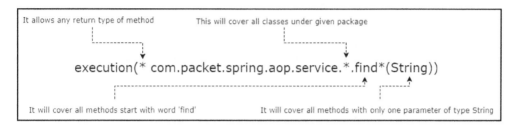

Declaring Advice (interceptor)

The next step is to define **Advice**. This is an action performed on a join-point. Advice is also referred as an *interceptor*. Spring AOP supports various types of Advice, as shown here:

- **Before Advice:** This type of Advice is executed just before the execution starts at the join-point. In the case of an exception, Spring will stop further execution of this Advice.
- **After Advice:** As its name suggests, this type of Advice is executed after completion of join-point execution (either a normal exit, or in the case of an exception, from the join-point).
- **Around Advice:** This type of Advice is executed around the join-point (before and/or after the advised method). Because of this, you have the control to execute the join-point and return the original method value, or bypass the flow and return a custom value. In general, around Advice is used to execute some logic before and/or after a method's main logic. Due to this, it's the most powerful type of Advice.
- **After returning Advice:** This is similar to after Advice. The difference is that it's being executed on a normal exit from a join-point.

- **After throwing Advice:** This is also similar to after Advice, but is executed when an exception occurred during execution of the Advice's method.

 In XML-based Spring AOP, you need to be careful of the order of AOP elements while defining them within `<aop:config>`. For example, `<aop:pointcut>` must be defined before or within the `<aop:aspect>` element or else Spring will show an error. Similarly, AOP Advice must be defined within the `<aop:aspect>` element.

Implementing before advice

So far we have seen how to declare aspects, point-cuts, and Advice. Let's put them together and understand how they work together. Suppose we want to put a logger at the beginning of all methods of classes that fall under the `com.packet.spring.aop.service` package. The configuration would be as follows:

```
<aop:config>
    <aop:pointcut id="employeeServiceMethods"
      expression="execution(* com.packet.spring.aop.service.*.*(..))" />
    <aop:aspect id="myLoggin" ref="loggingAspect">
        <aop:before pointcut-ref="employeeServiceMethods"
            method="printStartLog"/>
    </aop:aspect>
</aop:config>
<bean id="loggingAspect"
class="com.packet.spring.aop.aspects.LoggingAspect">
</bean>
<bean id="employeeService"
class="com.packet.spring.aop.service.EmployeeService">
</bean>
```

We have defined a point-cut that matches all public methods of all classes under the `com.packet.spring.aop.service` package, with any parameter and any return value. Next, we have defined the logging aspect bean, and given its reference to `<aop:aspect>` with the `ref` attribute.

Inside the aspect, we have defined before advice (`<aop:before>`) and gave point-cut reference there. The `printStartLog` method is defined in the aspect bean as follows:

```
package com.packt.spring.aop.aspects;

import org.aspectj.lang.JoinPoint;
public class LoggingAspect {
```

```
public void printStartLog(JoinPoint joinPoint) {
    System.out.println(" ****** Starting Method
'"+joinPoint.getSignature().getName()+"' of
"+joinPoint.getTarget().getClass());
    }
}
```

In this snippet, `printStartLog` is the advice method. It takes a parameter of type `JoinPoint`, which represents the join-points that we associated with the aspect. This class provides metadata about the target object, such as its method (on which this advice is woven), class, and other attributes.

It's not required to pass the `JoinPoint` parameter in the `printStartLog` method. It will work even if you don't pass the `JoinPoint` parameter. But, it gives you metadata about the target object. In this sense, it's useful. For example, in the previous case, we display the woven method's name and its class name.

The target class `EmployeeService` is defined in the `com.packet.spring.aop.service` package as follows:

```
package com.packt.spring.aop.service;

public class EmployeeService {

 public void generateSalarySlip() {
    System.out.println("Generating payslip");
  }
 public String showTotalEmployee(String test) {
    System.out.println(" The string is -->"+test);
    return test;
  }
 public void findEmployee(String employeeId) {
    System.out.println(" finding employee based on employeeId ");
  }
}
```

When we get the `EmployeeService` object from Spring's application context file and call these methods, AOP will intercept all these methods and insert the log (which we kept in the `printStartLog` of `LoggingAspect`), before execution of each of the methods (because we have used before advice):

```
package com.packt.spring.aop.aspects.main;

import org.springframework.context.ApplicationContext;
import org.springframework.context.support.ClassPathXmlApplicationContext;
```

```
import com.packet.spring.aop.report.api.IExportPaySlip;
import com.packet.spring.aop.service.EmployeeService;
import com.packet.spring.aop.service.HRService;

public class SpringAOPInXMLCheck {

  public static void main(String[] args) {
    ApplicationContext springContext = new
ClassPathXmlApplicationContext("application-context.xml");
    EmployeeService employeeService =
(EmployeeService)springContext.getBean("employeeService");
    employeeService.generateSalarySlip();
    employeeService.showTotalEmployee("test");
    employeeService.findEmployee("abc123");
  }
}
```

And you will get output as follows:

```
---------------------------------------------
 ****** Starting Method 'generateSalarySlip' of class
com.packet.spring.aop.service.EmployeeService
Generating payslip

 ****** Starting Method 'showTotalEmployee' of class
com.packet.spring.aop.service.EmployeeService
The string is -->test

 ****** Starting Method 'findEmployee' of class
com.packet.spring.aop.service.EmployeeService
 finding employee based on employeeId
```

You can observe how Spring AOP traps each method of the EmployeeService class and adds the log at the beginning of each method. It prints the method name and class name dynamically.

Implementing after advice

Just like before advice, we can also implement other advice types. Let's take an example of after advice and around advice. For after advice, just add one method in the `LoggingAspect` class as follows:

```
//After advice method.
  public void printEndLog(JoinPoint joinPoint) {
     System.out.println(" ****** End of Method
'"+joinPoint.getSignature().getName());
  }
```

In after advice, we are just printing the `method` name. We also need to update the aspect configuration in the application context file. Just add an after advice entry for our logging aspect, as follows:

```
<aop:aspect id="myLoggin" ref="loggingAspect">
      <aop:before pointcut-ref="employeeServiceMethods"
method="printStartLog"/>
      <aop:after pointcut-ref="employeeServiceMethods"
method="printEndLog"/>
</aop:aspect>
```

You will get the following output:

```
------------------------------------
 ****** Starting Method 'generateSalarySlip' of class
com.packet.spring.aop.service.EmployeeService
Generating payslip
 ****** End of Method 'generateSalarySlip'

 ****** Starting Method 'showTotalEmployee' of class
com.packet.spring.aop.service.EmployeeService
 The string is -->test
 ****** End of Method 'showTotalEmployee

 ****** Starting Method 'findEmployee' of class
com.packet.spring.aop.service.EmployeeService
 finding employee based on employeeId
 ****** End of Method 'findEmployee
```

This time, you can observe how AOP intercepts each method and implements after advice along with before advice.

Implementing around advice

Spring AOP also provides around advice, which is a combination of before and after in one go. If you need to process something before and after, you can simply implement around advice instead of before and after advice separately. To implement around advice, just add one more method in our LoggingAspect as follows:

```
//Around advice method.
  public void printAroundLog(ProceedingJoinPoint proceedingJointPoint)
throws Throwable {
    System.out.println("----- Starting of Method
"+proceedingJointPoint.getSignature().getName());
    proceedingJointPoint.proceed();
    System.out.println("----- ending of Method
"+proceedingJointPoint.getSignature().getName());
  }
```

For *around* advice, Spring AOP supplies the ProceedingJoinPoint object instead of JoinPoint object. proceedingJoinPoint.proceed() will simply call the method on the target object, and you can put the before logic just above the proceedingJoinPoint.proceed() call and after the logic just next to it.

 ProceedingJoinPoint can be used for around advice only. If you try to use it for before or after advice, you will get an error. For them, you should use join-point only.

The last step is to update the configuration to plug around advice for the aspect as follows:

```
<aop:aspect id="myLoggin" ref="loggingAspect">
        <aop:around pointcut-ref="employeeServiceMethods"
method="printAroundLog"/>
</aop:aspect>
```

You will get output as follows:

```
----------------------------------
----- Starting of Method generateSalarySlip
Generating payslip
----- ending of Method generateSalarySlip

----- Starting of Method showTotalEmployee
  The string is -->test
----- ending of Method showTotalEmployee
```

```
----- Starting of Method findEmployee
  finding employee based on employeeId
----- ending of Method findEmployee
```

This is how around advice is implemented and does the work of *before* and *after* advice altogether.

Don't use *before, after,* and *around* advice all together. If you need to put some additional code at the beginning of the method, use *before* advice only, instead of *around*. Although using *around* advice can achieve what you implemented with *before* advice alone, it's not a good idea. Use *around* advice only when you want to add something before and after methods.

Implementing after returning advice

The **after returning** advice works just like after advice. The only difference is that this advice will be executed on matching methods only on normal exit. If an exception occurs, this advice will not be applied.

We will look at a scenario to understand the need for this advice. Suppose you want to send a message (email) to a concerned person when a particular method is executed successfully on the `target` class. Since this is a new concern (sending a message on successful execution of the `target` method), we have created a new aspect class as follows:

```
package com.packt.spring.aop.aspects;
import org.aspectj.lang.JoinPoint;
public class SendMessage {

    //Advice method after successful existing of target method.
    public void sendMessageOnSuccessExit(JoinPoint joinPoint) {
        System.out.println(" ****** Method
'"+joinPoint.getSignature().getName()|"' of
"+joinPoint.getTarget().getClass()+" is executed successfully...");
    }
}
```

The SendMessage aspect has one method called sendMessageOnSuccessExit. We want this method to be called on a normal method exit (without an exception) from the target class. You can write the logic to send the message (email) in this method. The new aspect will be configured in the application context (XML) file as follows:

```xml
<aop:pointcut id="hrServiceMethods"
        expression="execution(*
com.packet.spring.aop.service.HRService.*(..))" />

<aop:aspect id="sendMsg" ref="sendMsgAspect">
      <aop:after-returning pointcut-ref="hrServiceMethods"
        method="sendMessageOnSuccessExit"/>
</aop:aspect>
```

We have created a new point-cut that will match all the methods of the HRService class. This class will be as follows:

```java
package com.packt.spring.aop.service;

public class HRService {
  public void showHolidayList() {
    System.out.println("This is holiday list method...");
  }

  public void showMyLeave() throws Exception {
    System.out.println("Showing employee leaves...");
    throw new Exception();
  }
}
```

When you get an object of HRService from Spring and call the showHolidayList method, you will get output as follows:

```
This is holiday list method...
 ****** Method 'showHolidayList' of class
com.packet.spring.aop.service.HRService is executed successfully...
```

If the `target` method returns a value and you want to modify it with AOP, you can do this with after returning advice. For this, you need to specify the parameter name in the `<aop:aspect>` element as follows:

```
<aop:aspect id="sendMsg" ref="sendMsgAspect">
    <aop:after-returning pointcut-ref="hrServiceMethods"
     returning="retVal"
     method="sendMessageOnSuccessExit"/>
</aop:aspect>
```

In this code, the value of the `returning` attribute says that the `sendMessageOnSuccessExit` method must declare a parameter called `retVal`. Spring AOP will pass the return value from the method of the `target` object to this parameter (`retVal`) while applying this advice. Therefore, the type of the return value from the method of the `target` object must be compatible with the type of the parameter (`retVal`, in our case) in the advice method. Let's update the `showHoliday` method of the `SendMessage` advice as follows:

```
public String showHolidayList() {
    System.out.println("This is holiday list method...");
    return "holidayList";
}
```

The return value type of this method is `String`. To update the return value, you need to change the advice method as follows:

```
//Advice method after successful existing of target method.
    public String sendMessageOnSuccessExit(JoinPoint joinPoint,String
retVal) {
        System.out.println(" ****** Method
'"+joinPoint.getSignature().getName()+"' of
"+joinPoint.getTarget().getClass()+" is executed successfully...");
        System.out.println(" The return value is -->"+retVal);
        return "Successfully exited with return val is -->"+retVal;
    }
```

When you get the `HRService` object from Spring and call its `showHolidayList()` method, you will get the following updated return value:

```
This is holiday list method...
 ****** Method 'showHolidayList' of class
com.packet.spring.aop.service.HRService is executed successfully...
 The return value is -->holidayList
```

Implementing AfterThrowing advice

The AfterThrowing advice will be executed when the matched methods of the target object exit with an exception. This is also useful when you want to take an action on an exception that occurred during execution of the method. Let's create AfterThrowing advice as follows:

```
<aop:aspect id="sendMsg" ref="sendMsgAspect">
  <aop:after-returning pointcut-ref="hrServiceMethods"
       returning="retVal" method="sendMessageOnSuccessExit"/>
  <aop:after-throwing pointcut-ref="hrServiceMethods"
       method="sendMessageOnErrorExit"/>
</aop:aspect>
```

The `sendMessageOnErrorExit` advice method will be defined in the `sendMessage` aspect as follows:

```
//Advice method on existing of target method with some error / exception
public void sendMessageOnErrorExit(JoinPoint joinPoint) {
    System.out.println(" ****** Method
'"+joinPoint.getSignature().getName()+"'
    of "+joinPoint.getTarget().getClass()+" has some error ...");
}
```

To make sure this advice is applied, the method in the `target` class must exist with an exception. So, let's add one method that throws an exception in the `target` class (HRService) as follows:

```
public void showMyLeave() throws Exception {
    System.out.println("Showing employee leaves...");
    throw new Exception();
}
```

When you take the `HRService` object from Spring and call the `showMyLeave` method, you will get output as follows:

```
Showing employee leaves...
 ****** Method 'showMyLeave' of class
com.packet.spring.aop.service.HRService has some error ...
java.lang.Exception
  at com.packet.spring.aop.service.HRService.showMyLeave(HRService.java:12)
  at
com.packet.spring.aop.service.HRService$$FastClassBySpringCGLIB$$a3eb49fe.i
nvoke(<generated>)
...
```

@AspectJ annotation-based Spring AOP

Spring allows another way to support AOP through the @AspectJ annotation. It's an alternative to XML-based configuration to define the aspect using regular Java classes with AOP-specific annotation. Spring introduced the @AspectJ style as a part of the AspectJ 5 release. Though with @AspectJ, Spring facilitates same annotation like AspectJ 5, the underlying framework is pure Spring AOP. Due to this arrangement, there is no dependency on AspectJ compiler or weaver.

To use @AspectJ annotation for Spring AOP, you need to enable its support in Spring through configuration and turn auto-proxy on. **Autoproxying** is a mechanism to create a proxy on the object of a Spring bean on which one or more aspects are woven. This allows Spring AOP to intercept the methods and apply advice on the matching point-cut.

As we have seen in `Chapter 3`, *Dependency Injection with Spring*, Spring supports configuration of annotation either in the application context (XML) file, or in the Java configuration. Similarly, @AspectJ configuration can be done with either of these options. With Java-based configuration, you can enable Spring AOP annotation with the following code:

```
@Configuration
@EnableAspectJAutoProxy
public class SpringConfig {

}
```

Alternatively, you can choose the application context (XML) file to enable `@Aspect` annotation. This can be achieved with the `<aop:aspectj-autoproxy/>` element.

 Spring AOP creates a proxy object to embed customer code; however, when you define any class as an aspect with the @Aspect annotation (or XML configuration), Spring will not create the proxy of that class. In short, the aspect class can't be the target of advice from another aspect. Spring will omit all such aspect classes from auto-proxy.

Declaring aspect

The concept of declaring Aspect with the @AspectJ annotation style is somewhat similar to XML schema-based AOP declaration. Just to recall, a Java class can be an Aspect in the Spring AOP framework. In annotation-based Spring AOP, you can declare any bean as an Aspect with the `@Aspect` annotation as follows:

```
package com.packt.spring.aop.aspects;
import org.aspectj.lang.annotation.Aspect;
import org.aspectj.lang.annotation.Pointcut;

@Aspect
public class SessionCheck {
}
```

The `SessionCheck` class is defined as a regular Spring bean in the application context (XML) file as follows:

```
<aop:aspectj-autoproxy/>
<bean id="sessionCheckAspect"
class="com.packt.spring.aop.aspects.SessionCheck">
</bean>
```

Aspect classes may have methods and fields like any other Java class. Spring doesn't impose any limits on defining aspects only with the bean defined in the application context (XML) file. If you have used bean autodetection through Java package scanning (with the `<context:component-scan>` element), Spring intelligently detects the `Aspect` class with the `@Aspect` annotation. Aspect classes may contain point-cuts and advice declaration.

> The @Aspect annotation itself is not sufficient for Spring to autodetect the class. You still need to use @Component, or any other stereotype annotation. @Aspect will consider the class (which is autodetected by @Component or an equivalent annotation) as an aspect for Spring AOP.

Declaring point-cut

Point-cuts are regular expressions or patterns to filter join-points where we want to apply advice. Since Spring AOP only supports method-level join-points, you can consider a point-cut as a matching of method execution on Spring beans. In the `@AspectJ` annotation style, a point-cut is declared by a method of an Aspect class (declared with the `@Aspect` annotation). Such methods are called **point-cut signatures**. The `@Pointcut` annotation is used to define such a method as follows:

```
@Aspect
public class SessionCheck {
   @Pointcut("execution( * com.packt.spring.aop.service.*.*(..))") //
Expression
   private void validateSession() {// Point-cut signature
   }
}
```

In this code, the `validateSession` method represents a point-cut signature, while the `@Pointcut` annotation is used to describe a point-cut expression. The preceding point-cut is applied to all public methods of all classes under the `com.packt.spring.aop.service` package that have any parameters and return values. A method that represents a point-cut signature must have `void` as a return type. The preceding annotation-based AOP is equivalent to XML-based AOP configuration, as follows:

```
<aop:config>
    <!-- point cut declaration   -->
    <aop:pointcut id="checkValidUser"
        expression="execution(* com.packet.spring.aop.service.*.*(..))" />

    <!-- aspect configuration   -->
    <aop:aspect id="mySessionCheck" ref="checkSessionAspect">
       //Advice declaration goes here.
    </aop:aspect>

    <!-- spring bean represents an aspect   -->
    <bean id="checkSessionAspect"
            class="com.packet.spring.aop.aspects.SessionCheck">
    </bean>
</aop:config>
```

Just like XML-based AOP, you can use various point-cut types (point-cut designators) such as `within`, `this`, `target`, `args`, `@annotation`, `@target`, `@within`, and `@args` with annotation-style AOP. On top of these, Spring supports an additional point-cut type (PCD) called **bean**, which matches the method execution on a particular bean or set of beans. It can be declared as follows:

```
@Pointcut("bean(batchOperation)")
    private void captureBatchProcess() {
    }
```

This point-cut is applied to the bean with an ID or name of `batchOperation` defined in the application context (XML) file. If a wildcard (only `*` is allowed) is used, this point-cut can be applied on multiple beans.

Just like XML-based configuration, annotation-based AOP also supports combining point-cut with `and`, `or`, and `negated` operations. In `@AspectJ`-style AOP, you can refer point-cut with its name (signature) while combining with other point-cut, or referring them in Aspect declaration in XML schema. Multiple point-cuts can be combined as follows:

```
@Pointcut("execution( * com.packt.spring.aop.report.*.*(..))")
private void checkSession() {
}

@Pointcut("args(String)")
private void printUserName() {
}

@Pointcut("checkSession() && printUserName()")
private void userSession() {
}
```

The first point-cut, `checkSession`, will be applied on all public methods of any class under the `com.packt.spring.aop.report` package. The second point-cut, `printUserName`, will be applied on any public method with a single argument of type `String`, while the third point-cut, `userSession`, is applicable on all public methods that have a single argument of type `String` of any classes under the `com.packt.spring.aop.report` package. We have used the name (point-cut signature) of the first and second point-cuts to combine them in the third point-cut definition.

It's common practice to create smaller point-cuts with simple expressions, and build complex point-cuts by combining them with `and`, `or`, and `negated` operations. By referring to its name, point-cuts are so simple to define, and yet powerful when combining with other point-cuts.

Since point-cuts are referred by `method` name, the visibility of the Java method is applied to point-cuts. For example, **private** point-cuts are used in the same type, **protected** point-cuts in the same package, and **public** point-cuts can be applied anywhere (that is, can be referred to in other aspect classes in different hierarchies). This brings great flexibility when building an enterprise application with multiple modules, and when you want to share a set of operations between various aspects. You can make public point-cuts in common aspects that can be shared with other aspects in different modules.

Declaring Advice

Declaring Advice with `@AspectJ`-style annotation is similar to XML-based AOP configuration. The XML configuration will be replaced by an annotation declaration in the aspect class. Just to recall, Advice is an action to be performed on a point-cut configured with it. Advice can be declared in the Aspect class as follows:

```
@Before("execution(* com.packt.spring.aop.report.*.*(..))")
public void displayUserName() {
   System.out.println(" Displaying the user name of logged in user --");
}
```

The `@Before` annotation is used to declare before advice with the `displayUserName` method. The point-cut expression defined within the `@Before` annotation is called *in-lined*, because it's declared in the same place. You can also put a reference of the point-cut (declared separately with the `@Pointcut` annotation) within the `@Before` annotation as follows:

```
@Pointcut("execution( * com.packt.spring.aop.report.*.*(..))")
private void checkSession() {
}

@Before("checkSession()")
public void displayUserName() {
    System.out.println(" Displaying the user name of logged in user --");
}
```

This is how a point-cut with the `method` **signature** `checkSession()` is being referred to in the `@Before` advice. The previous configuration is equivalent to the following XML-based configuration:

```
<aop:config>
    <!-- point cut declaration  -->
    <aop:pointcut id="checkSessionPointcut"
        expression="execution( * com.packt.spring.aop.report.*.*(..))" />

    <!-- aspect and advice configuration  -->
    <aop:aspect id="mySessionCheck" ref="checkSessionAspect">
        <aop:before pointcut-ref="checkSessionPointcut"
            method="displayUserName"/>
    </aop:aspect>

    <!-- spring bean represents an aspect  -->
    <bean id="checkSessionAspect"
            class="com.packet.spring.aop.aspects.SessionCheck">
    </bean>
</aop:config>
```

As we have seen, the access modifier of the point-cut signature will decide its visibility. You can refer any public point-cut to the advice on a different `Aspect` class as follows:

```
//New Aspect class.
@Aspect
public class PermissionCheck {
  @Pointcut("within(com.packt.spring.aop.report.*)")
  public void checkReportPermission() {
  }
}

//Define After advice within SessionCheck aspect class.
@After("com.packt.spring.aop.aspects.PermissionCheck.checkReportPermission(
)")
public void checkResourcePermission() {
  System.out.println("This is resource permission checker ..");
}
```

This is how you can refer to a public point-cut defined in some other aspect class. You need to use a fully-qualified class and put the `method` name with a dot in between. We have seen an example of before and after advice types. You can define other advice types, such as around advice, after returning advice and after throwing advice, similar to the schema-based AOP we have seen in previous topics.

Declaring an advisor

Spring provides another mechanism to define advice and aspect as a single unit. It's called an **advisor**. It's only available in Spring AOP and not in native AspectJ. In this model, you need to define advice as a class that implements one of the advice interfaces. An advisor can be defined with the `<aop:advisor>` element in the application context (XML) file as follows:

```
<aop:config>
        <aop:pointcut id="loggingPointcut" expression="execution(*
                com.packt.spring.aop.dao.*.*(..))" />
        <aop:advisor advice-ref="loggingAdvice"
                pointcut-ref="loggingPointcut" id="loggingInterceptorAdvisor" />
</aop:config>

<bean id="loggingAdvice"
class="com.packt.spring.aop.advisor.LoggingAdvisor" />
```

You need to define an advisor with the `<aop:advisor>` element within `<aop:config>`. You can define a point-cut advisor with the `point-cut-ref` attribute. In the previous example, we have defined an in-lined point-cut. If you are following annotation-based AOP, you can refer to any public point-cut defined in the aspect class as follows:

```
<aop:advisor advice-ref="loggingAdvice"
        pointcut-ref=
"com.packt.spring.aop.aspects.PermissionCheck.checkReportPermission()"
id="loggingInterceptorAdvisor" />
```

In this example, we are referring to the point-cut with its signature (`checkReportPermission()`) defined in the `PermissionCheck` aspect class.

We also defined a bean with the `LoggingAdvisor` class, which is an `advisor` class, and referred in the `<aop:advisor>` element with the `advice-ref` attribute. The `LogginAdvisor` class is defined as follows:

```
public class LoggingAdvisor implements MethodBeforeAdvice {
  @Override
  public void before(Method method, Object[] args, Object target) throws
    Throwable {
    System.out.println("****************** Starting "+method.getName()+"
method
    ****************");
  }
}
```

This `advisor` class is implementing the `before` method of the `MethodBeforeAdvise` interface. It's equivalent to implementing before advice. Spring AOP provides other sets of advice interfaces, such as `MethodInterceptor`, `ThrowsAdvice`, and `AfterReturningAdvice`, which are equivalent to implementing around advice, after throwing advice, and after returning advice respectively.

Choosing AOP frameworks and style of configuration

Once you conclude that you will go ahead with the Aspect programming model to achieve or implement your requirements, this question comes into the picture: should you choose Spring AOP or the full-fledged AspectJ framework ?

After choosing the framework, the question of selecting the style of configuration would come up next. For example, in the case of the AspectJ framework, will you choose AspectJ code style or @AspectJ annotation style? Similarly, in the case of Spring AOP, will you select a Spring XML file or an @AspectJ-based annotation style to define various artifacts such as aspects, point-cuts, advice, and advisors?

Choosing the right framework with the specific style for defining the configuration depends on many factors, such as project requirements, availability of development tools, team expertise, compatibility of your existing system code with the AOP framework, how quickly you want to implement AOP, and performance overhead.

Spring AOP versus AspectJ language

In this chapter, we mainly looked at Spring AOP. AspectJ is another solution to implement AOP; however, Spring AOP is simpler than AspectJ because it doesn't require you to introduce an AspectJ compiler or weaver into your development and build process.

Spring AOP has been introduced to provide a simple AOP implementation throughout the IoC container to solve generic problems, while AspectJ is a full featured AOP framework. AspectJ is powerful in nature, but more complex than Spring AOP. AspectJ supports compile-time, post-compile-time, and runtime weaving, while Spring AOP only supports runtime weaving through a proxy.

If your business needs advice on the set of operations of the Spring bean project, Spring AOP is the right choice for you. If you come across a requirement where you need to intercept and implement advice on objects not managed by the Spring container, you should go with the AspectJ programming framework.

Spring AOP supports method-level join-points only. If you need any advice on join-points other than methods (such as field, setter, or getter methods), you should consider AspectJ. Another point you should consider while choosing from these frameworks is performance. Spring AOP uses a proxy, so there should be little runtime overhead. Compared to Spring AOP, there is less overhead while working with AspectJ.

XML versus @AspectJ-style annotation for Spring AOP

When there is more than one option to choose from, it's always a dilemma, and that is the case here. Which option should you choose while using Spring AOP: XML-based or annotation-based? Each of these styles has benefits and limitations. You should consider them both before choosing the right one for your needs.

The XML style is very well-known and has been widely used since the evolution of the Spring Framework. Almost all Spring developers are handy with it. Choosing the XML style means all your configurations are in one central place. This will help to identify how many artifacts (aspects, point-cuts, and sets of advice) are defined in the system in a cleaner way. This will be a benefit in the alteration of the configuration (for example, changing the expression of a point-cut) independently.

On the other hand, with the XML style, a piece of information is split across different places. The configuration is done in XML, while the actual implementation is defined in the respective bean classes. While using @AspectJ-style annotation, there will be just a single module, Aspect, which declares that all the artifacts, such as point-cuts, advice, and so on, are well encapsulated.

There are other limitations to XML based AOP, for example, a bean declared as an Aspect would be a singleton only. Also, you can't refer to the point-cut by its signature (name) while combining with other point-cuts. To take an example, a point-cut declaration with an annotation is as follows:

```
@Pointcut("execution( * com.packt.spring.aop.report.*.*(..))")
private void checkSession() {
}
@Pointcut("args(String)")
private void printUserName() {
}
@Pointcut("checkSession() && printUserName()")
private void userSession() {
}
```

The point-cut signatures (names) of checkSession and printUserName are used to combine them and form a new expression, userSession. The downside of XML-based configuration is that you can't combine point-cut expressions like this.

On top of these facts, Spring AOP allows you to mix XML schema-based configuration with @AspectJ-style annotation declaration. For example, you can define a point-cut and an aspect with annotation, and declare the set of advice (interceptors) in XML-based configuration. They all can coexist without any issues.

Summary

In this chapter, we learned one of the important ways to achieve separation of concerns called AOP. Conceptually, we are removing the dependency of cross-cutting concerns from business code and applying them with plug-and -play fashion and in a more controlled way with AOP. It solves the design problem that we never could resolve with the traditional AOP model.

We understood the need of AOP by taking an example where we need to keep changing business code when common functionality is changed. We have also seen various terminologies used in AOP, which is very crucial to understanding underlying concepts.

Soon after learning the theory of AOP, we started our journey with Spring AOP to understand the practical concepts. First, we learned to define AOP configuration in an XML file, followed by declaring various artifacts such as aspect, point-cut, and advice. Details about point-cut expressions and advice types were shown with various examples and code samples.

Next, we learned how to define Spring AOP configuration with the `@AspectJ` annotation style, followed by declaring aspects, advice, and point-cuts with annotation. We also learned how to define an advisor by implementing various interfaces. Lastly, we saw the benefits and limitations of Spring AOP and the AspectJ framework, followed by how to choose the configuration style for Spring AOP: XML or annotation.

We will move on to learn various design patterns that you can use to achieve IoC, and what the best practices, patterns, and anti-patterns are while working with dependency injection in the next chapter.

IoC Patterns and Best Practices 7

Now that you have reached this chapter, you should know what **Dependency Injection (DI)** is, why it's so important, how it's projected in recent versions of Java, and how to implement it with popular frameworks, such as Spring and Google Guice, with various scopes.

It's said that knowing something is not enough until it's applied with best methodologies and practices. Knowledge is power only when it's implemented in the right manner. An improper approach may create a big mess.

The software industry is moving toward modularity. The concepts of DI and **Inversion of Control (IoC)** containers were created due to this, and this is why they are so popular today. Still, many developers don't know how to utilize DI to its full potential.

In this chapter, we will explore the real strength of DI by learning the right patterns and best practices to apply the expertise we gained in DI in previous chapters. This chapter is not meant to do anything new; instead, we will learn how to do things in the right manner.

In this chapter, we will cover the following topics:

- Various patterns to achieve IoC
- Configuration styles
- Injection using the setter method versus constructor
- Circular dependency
- Best practices and anti-patterns

Various patterns to achieve IoC

Let's recall what the **Dependency Inversion Principle (DIP)** states: high-level modules should not depend upon low-level modules; both should depend upon abstraction. This is a fundamental requirement for making any application modular and adjustable.

While designing any system, we should make sure that high-level classes do not instantiate low-level classes; instead, they should rely on abstraction (the interface or abstract class) rather than depending on other concrete classes directly. The DIP does not specify how this happens, so a technique is required to separate the low-level modules from the high-level modules. IoC provides this technique.

There are various patterns to achieve IoC, including inverting the object creation process from your class to some other class and reducing the coupling between modules or classes. Let's discuss these patterns, focusing more on how they decouple the modules and achieve separation of concerns:

- The factory method pattern
- The service locator pattern
- The template method pattern
- The strategy pattern

All of these patterns encapsulate a specific responsibility, which makes the system modular.

The factory method pattern

The factory method pattern concerns defining an interface (or abstract class) method for creating dependency objects. This method is called a factory method. The class (or interface) that holds the factory method will be considered an abstract creator. The actual object creation process does not happen in the factory method directly.

The concrete creators (which implement the factory method) will decide which dependent class to instantiate. In short, the dependent object is decided at runtime. This process has been described in the following diagram:

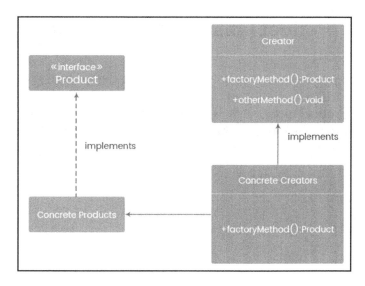

The factory pattern's implementation is a four-step process:

1. Declaring the product (the abstract product type).
2. Creating the concrete product.
3. Defining the factory method – a creator.
4. Creating concrete creators (concrete subclasses).

Let's understand these steps by using an example. Suppose you are developing an application for a message service provider. Initially, the company provides an SMS service for cellular devices. So, the first version of your application code is handling message distribution with SMS only, assuming that the bulk of code is written in the SMS class.

Gradually, the service becomes popular and you want to add other bulk message services, such as email, WhatsApp, and other social media message services. This requires code changes because you have added all the code to the SMS class. This change in code is required for every new messaging service that is introduced into the system in future.

The factory method pattern suggests that the solution to this problem will be inverting the object creation process from the client code (with a new operator) to a specific method: the factory method. The factory method defines a common interface that returns an abstract product type. A concrete product's creation is done in the child classes, which implement the factory method. The objects returned from the factory method are referred to as **Product** in the preceding diagram. First, let's define an abstract product type and its concrete implementation for the preceding example.

Defining the product (abstract type) and its concrete implementation

In our case, the **MessageApp** interface represents an abstract product type. The implementation of each messaging app would reside in their respective concrete classes, which are concrete product types, such as **SMSMessage**, **EmailMessage**, and **WhatsAppMessage**. This relationship is described with the following diagram:

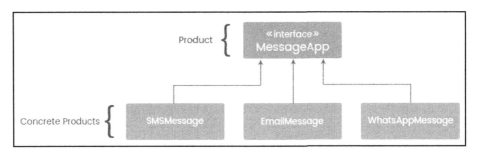

The product (abstract type) and all of the concrete product classes should look as follows:

```
// Product (abstract type)
public interface MessageApp {
  void sendMessage(String message);
}

//Concrete Product
public class EmailMessage implements MessageApp {
  @Override
  public void sendMessage(String message) {
    //Mail specific implementation
    System.out.println("Sending eMail message ...."+message);
  }
}

//Concrete Product
public class SMSMessage implements MessageApp {
  @Override
  public void sendMessage(String message) {
    //SMS specific implementation.
    System.out.println("sending SMS message ..."+message);
  }
}

//Concrete Product
public class WhatsAppMessage implements MessageApp {
```

```
@Override
public void sendMessage(String message) {
  //Whatsapp specific implementation
  System.out.println("Sending Whatsapp message ..."+message);
}
}
```

Defining the factory method (creator interface) and its concrete implementation

The next step is to create a class and define the factory method that returns the abstract product type (**MessageApp**, in our case). This class is considered an abstract creator. The factory method would be in the form of either an interface or the abstract method. All concrete creators must implement this factory method. The following diagram describes the complete relationship between these components:

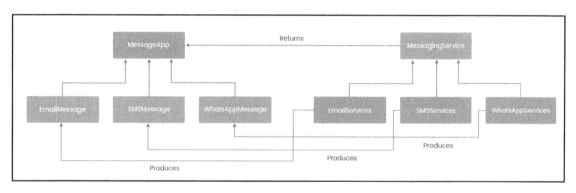

Here, **MessagingService** is the creator, while **EmailServices**, **SMSServices**, and **WhatsAppServices** are concrete creators. Each concrete creator produces the respective concrete product type.

The factory method and its concrete implementation classes should look as follows:

```
//Abstract creator
public abstract class MessagingService {
  //This is Factory method.
  public abstract MessageApp createMessageApp();
}

//Concrete creator
public class EmailServices extends MessagingService{
  @Override
```

```
    public MessageApp createMessageApp() {
      return new EmailMessage();
    }
}

//Concrete creator
public class SMSServices extends MessagingService {
  @Override
  public MessageApp createMessageApp() {
    return new SMSMessage();
  }
}

//Concrete creator
public class WhatsAppServices extends MessagingService {
  @Override
  public MessageApp createMessageApp() {
    return new WhatsAppMessage();
  }
}
```

 In the preceding case, we have used an abstract class, but you can also use an interface for the factory method (abstract creator). If you are planning to provide any common methods, you can choose an abstract class, or else an interface would be an appropriate choice.

Finally, the factory class that provided the specific implementation looks as follows:

```
public class MessagingFactory {
  public MessageApp getMessageApp(MessageType messageType) {
    MessageApp messageApp = null;
    // 1.Based on messageType value, create concrete implementation.
    // 2.Call factory method on each of them to get abstract product type -
MessageApp in our case
    // 3.call common method on abstract product type to execute desire
operation.
    switch(messageType) {
    case SMSType:
      messageApp = new SMSServices().createMessageApp();
      break;
    case EmailType:
      messageApp = new EmailServices().createMessageApp();
      break;
    case WhatsAppType:
      messageApp = new WhatsAppServices().createMessageApp();
      break;
    default: System.out.println(" Unknown message type .. Please provide
```

```
valid message type ");
      }
      return messageApp;
   }
}
```

This class returns the concrete implementation based on a specific `enum` type. The following code snippet depicts how client code can use the factory method:

```
public class Client {
   public static void main(String[] args) {
      MessagingFactory messagingFactory = new MessagingFactory();
      MessageApp smsApp =
messagingFactory.getMessageApp(MessageType.SMSType);
      MessageApp emailApp =
messagingFactory.getMessageApp(MessageType.EmailType);
      MessageApp whatsAppApp =
messagingFactory.getMessageApp(MessageType.WhatsAppType);
      smsApp.sendMessage(" Hello ");
      emailApp.sendMessage(" this is test ");
      whatsAppApp.sendMessage(" Good Morning");
   }
}
```

This is described with the following diagram:

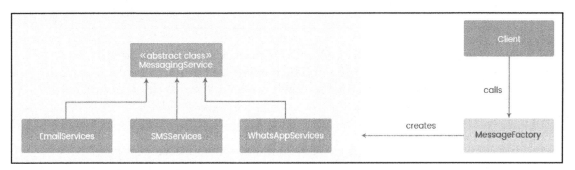

With the factory method pattern, you can make the product creation process abstracted from the client class. This way, the factory method pattern removes the dependency of the concrete product classes from the rest of the system. Additionally, the factory method delegates the actual object creation process to concrete creators. As long as the client code knows the type, the factory class will supply the dependency object of that type. This way, the factory method allows client code to depend on abstraction rather than concrete implementation. This is how IoC is achieved through the factory method pattern.

The service locator pattern

The service locator pattern entails removing dependencies from the client object by introducing a mediator. The client object will talk to the mediator to get a desired dependency. We will call this mediator the service locator, or just the locator.

The service locator involves the process of obtaining services with the abstract layer. Ideally, the locator should hold all the services (dependencies) and provide them with a single interface. It is a kind of central repository to find a service, usually by a string or interface type.

The service locator describes how to register and locate the service rather than telling us how to instantiate it. It lets the application register the concrete implementation for the given contract. You can add services either programmatically or through configuration. The implementation of the service locator is described in the following diagram:

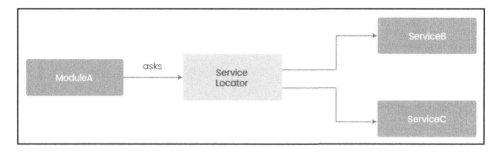

This is a very simple form of the service locator pattern. **ModuleA** is dependent on **ServiceB** and **ServiceC**, which are provided by the **Service Locator**. However, you can make the **Service Locator** more abstract so that it can handle any type of service. Let's understand how to do that.

It is always a good idea to expose any service with an interface. We will take an example of two such service interfaces and their implementations in the following snippet:

```
public interface CompressionAlgorithm {
  void doCompress();
}
public interface EncryptionAlgorithm {
  void doEncryption();
}

public class RARCompression implements CompressionAlgorithm {
  @Override
  public void doCompress() {
```

```
      System.out.println(" Compressing in RAR format ... ");
    }
  }

  public class ZIPCompression implements CompressionAlgorithm {
    @Override
    public void doCompress() {
      System.out.println(" Compressing in ZIP format ... ");
    }
  }
```

We want to get compression and encryption services from the service locator. We will write the ServiceLocator class, which is a singleton, and allows us to register these services. Once this is done, the client can get the services by the type of service interface. The ServiceLocator class will look as follows:

```
public class ServiceLocator {
  // Map which holds all services.
  private Map<Class<?>,Map<String,Object>> serviceRegistry = new
HashMap<Class<?>,Map<String,Object>>();
  private static ServiceLocator serviceLocator;
  // private constructor to make this class singleton
  private ServiceLocator() {
  }
  //Static method to get only existing instance. If no instance is there,
create the new one.
  public static ServiceLocator getInstance() {
    if(serviceLocator == null) {
      serviceLocator = new ServiceLocator();
    }
    return serviceLocator;
  }
  public <T> void registerService(Class<T> interfaceType, String key,
Object serviceObject) {
    Map<String,Object> serviceOfSameTypeMap =
serviceRegistry.get(interfaceType);
    if(serviceOfSameTypeMap !=null) {
      serviceRegistry.get(interfaceType).put(key, serviceObject);
    }else {
      serviceOfSameTypeMap = new HashMap<String,Object>();
      serviceOfSameTypeMap.put(key, serviceObject);
      serviceRegistry.put(interfaceType, serviceOfSameTypeMap);
    }
  }
  public <T> T getSerivce(Class<T> interfaceType, String key) {
    Map<String,Object> serviceOfSameTypeMap =
serviceRegistry.get(interfaceType);
```

```
      if(serviceOfSameTypeMap != null) {
        T service = (T)serviceOfSameTypeMap.get(key);
        if(service !=null) {
          return service;
        }else {
          System.out.println(" Service with key "+ key +" does not exist");
          return null;
        }
      }else {
        System.out.println(" Service of type "+ interfaceType.toString() + "
  does not exist");
        return null;
      }
    }
  }
}
```

It is not mandatory to use the interface for registering the services, but it is good practice. In future, if any new service of the same interface is introduced or a completely new set of services of a brand new interface is introduced, they can be easily accommodated without affecting the client code.

Also, with an interface, client code is more generic and you can change the implementation just by changing the key, making the system more flexible and loosely coupled. Finally, the service locator is used in client code, as you can see in the following snippet:

```
public class ServiceLocatorDemo {

  public static void main(String[] args) {
    ServiceLocator locator = ServiceLocator.getInstance();
    initializeAndRegisterServices(locator);
    CompressionAlgorithm rarCompression =
locator.getSerivce(CompressionAlgorithm.class, "rar");
    rarCompression.doCompress();
    CompressionAlgorithm zipCompression =
locator.getSerivce(CompressionAlgorithm.class, "zip");
    zipCompression.doCompress();
    EncryptionAlgorithm rsaEncryption =
locator.getSerivce(EncryptionAlgorithm.class, "rsa");
    rsaEncryption.doEncryption();
    EncryptionAlgorithm aesEncryption =
locator.getSerivce(EncryptionAlgorithm.class, "aes");
    aesEncryption.doEncryption();
  }
  private static void initializeAndRegisterServices( ServiceLocator locator
) {
    CompressionAlgorithm rarCompression = new RARCompression();
    CompressionAlgorithm zipCompression = new ZIPCompression();
```

```
    EncryptionAlgorithm rsaEncryption = new RSAEncrption();
    EncryptionAlgorithm aesEncryption = new AESEncrption();
    locator.registerService(CompressionAlgorithm.class, "rar",
rarCompression);
    locator.registerService(CompressionAlgorithm.class, "zip",
zipCompression);
    locator.registerService(EncryptionAlgorithm.class, "rsa",
rsaEncryption);
    locator.registerService(EncryptionAlgorithm.class, "aes",
aesEncryption);
  }
}
```

The service locator decouples the classes from their dependencies. The direct benefit of this arrangement is that the dependency can be replaced with little or (ideally) no code change. This way, the service locator pattern inverts the flow of control from the client code to the locator component. This is how IoC is implemented.

> In the service locator pattern, you need to make sure that all services are readily available before your objects start consuming it.

At first glance, it looks like the factory method pattern and service locator pattern work similarly. However, there are a few differences, as follows:

- **Construction cost:** If the class instantiation process inside the factory method is very expensive (in terms of resource consumption), then creating a new object in the factory method will result in performance issues. In short, the cost of construction in the factory method may impact overall system performance. In the service locator pattern, all of the dependency objects are created (ideally) during the application startup. The client can get the dependency service from a pre-instantiated registry.
- **Existing versus new objects:** Sometimes, you need same object every time. In the factory method pattern, we are returning a new instance every time, while the service locator pattern returns an existing instance of the dependency service to the caller.
- **Ownership:** Since the factory class returns a fresh new instance to the caller, the ownership lies with the caller class, whereas the service locator locates and returns an existing instance of the service, and so the ownership of the returned objects would be with the service locator.

The template method pattern

The template method pattern involves defining the common structure of an algorithm, and then allowing subclasses to change or redefine some portion of the algorithm without changing the complete structure. In other words, the template method pattern defines a function in a set of operations, allowing subclasses to redefine a few steps without altering the complete structure.

In this pattern, the base class declares the generic procedure with placeholders and lets subclasses provide the specific implementations of those placeholders while keeping the overall structure unchanged.

Let's understand the template method pattern with an example. Suppose you are writing a program to take row data, validate it, format it, and insert it into a database. Initially, the row data is provided in a CSV file, so you have created a class called `ProcessCSVData`. This class contains the logic for the following steps:

1. Reading the CSV file
2. Validating data
3. Formatting data
4. Inserting the data into the database

A year later, a few more formats of raw data are introduced, such as HTML, XML, text, and Excel. For each of these formats, if you a create separate class, you will end up having lots of similar code. It is obvious that each of these classes is quite different in file formats, while their other logic of data validation, formation, and insertion into the database is identical among them.

Think about the client code where these classes are used. You need to provide lots of `if...else` conditions to choose a specific implementation. This is not a good design. To achieve reusability, it is essential to get rid of code duplication and make the algorithm structure unbroken. If all of these classes are sharing a common base class, this problem can be solved by using polymorphism.

To implement the template method pattern, you need to identify which steps of the algorithm are common and which are variants or customizable in nature. The common steps should be implemented in the base class, while the variant steps should be placed in the base class with either the default implementation or no implementation at all. The variant steps will be considered as placeholder or extension points that must be supplied by a concrete-derived class.

In our example, reading data from a file is the only varying step, so we will keep it in the base class with default (or no) implementation in the method. This is considered as a template method. All concrete subclasses must provide implementations of this template method (reading the file from the respective formats). Other steps, such as validating, formatting, and inserting into the database, are common or invariant, so keep them in the base class as is. This implementation is described by the following diagram:

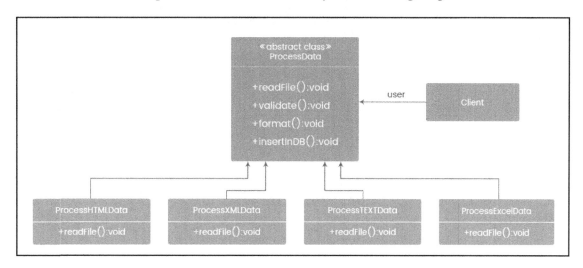

The following code snippet represents this implementation:

```
public abstract class ProcessData {
   //Template method
   public abstract void readFile();
   public void validate() {
      System.out.println(" Validating data ..");
   }
   public void format() {
      System.out.println(" Formatting data ..");
   }
   public void insertInDB() {
      System.out.println(" Inserting data into Database ..");
   }
}
```

The implementation's subclasses should look as follows:

```
public class ProcessExcelData extends ProcessData{
  @Override
  public void readFile() {
    System.out.println(" Reading Excel file");
  }
}

public class ProcessHTMLData extends ProcessData{
  @Override
  public void readFile() {
    System.out.println(" Reading HTML file");
  }
}

public class ProcessTEXTData extends ProcessData{
  @Override
  public void readFile() {
    System.out.println(" Reading Text file");
  }
}

public class ProcessXMLData extends ProcessData{
  @Override
  public void readFile() {
    System.out.println(" Reading Excel file");
  }
}
```

Finally, the client code that uses the template method should look as follows:

```
public class TemplateDemo {

  public static void main(String args[]) {
    ProcessData processData = new ProcessExcelData();
    processData.readFile();
    processData.validate();
    processData.format();
    processData.insertInDB();
    processData = new ProcessHTMLData();
    processData.readFile();
    processData.validate();
    processData.format();
    processData.insertInDB();
  }
}
```

We have used just two subclasses in client code. Similarly, you can use the remaining two subclasses. You will get the following output:

```
Reading Excel file
Validating data ..
Formatting data ..
Inserting data into Database ..
Reading HTML file
Validating data ..
Formatting data ..
Inserting data into Database ..
```

The template method pattern allows the framework to define invariant pieces of the program and to specify the hook or placeholder for all possible customization options. This way, the framework becomes the center point of the product, while the customization is considered as an additional capability or add-on on top of the core functionality.

The customization written for each of the template methods will get common functionalities from a generic framework or component. In other words, each client's customization receives the flow of control from the generic framework. The inverted control mechanism has been affectionately named the Hollywood Principle – "do not call us, we will call you". This is how IoC is achieved through the template method pattern.

The strategy pattern

The strategy pattern defines a set of algorithms, encapsulates each of them, and makes them interchangeable at runtime. This pattern lets the implementation vary independently from the clients that use it. In short, you can change the output of a class by changing the algorithm at runtime. The strategy pattern focuses on creating an interface with different implementations that follows the same behavioral contract.

Let's understand this pattern with an example. Suppose you are developing an application to upload documents into the cloud. Initially, you have been provided with a Google Drive upload. You probably wrote the `GoogleDriveCloud` class and put all of the logic in that.

At a later stage, you decided to support uploading documents on a few more cloud platforms, such as Dropbox, OneDrive, and Amazon S3. At this moment in time, you write separate classes for each of them, such as `DropboxCloud`, `OneDriveCloud`, and `AmazoneS3Cloud`.

All of these classes are used to upload documents onto the respective cloud. When you use them in your code, you will probably write the code to choose a specific implementation based on some condition.

In the preceding case, the `CloudUpload` class is tightly coupled with each of the cloud implementations, which is not a good design. You can think about the problems when you try to accommodate more cloud support in future. Every new implementation requires a change to the `CloudUpload` class. This is a clear violation of the open-closes principle: which talks about **open for extension but closed for modification**.

This situation can be mitigated with the strategy pattern. The pattern involves defining a set of related algorithms (implementations of various cloud platforms) and encapsulating them in classes that are separate from the host class (`CloudUpload`). The solution is described with the following diagram:

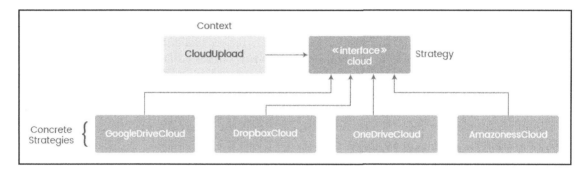

The implementation of the preceding diagram will look as follows:

```
//Interface
public interface Cloud {
   void upload();
}

//Concrete Algorithm
public class GoogleDriveCloud implements Cloud {
   @Override
   public void upload() {
      System.out.println(" Uploading on Google Drive ");
   }
}

//Concrete Algorithm
public class DropboxCloud implements Cloud {
   @Override
```

```
  public void upload() {
    System.out.println(" Uploading on Dropbox ");
  }
}

//Concrete Algorithm
public class OneDriveCloud implements Cloud {
  @Override
  public void upload() {
    System.out.println(" Uploading on OneDrive ");
  }
}

//Concrete Algorithm
public class AmazoneS3Cloud implements Cloud {
  @Override
  public void upload() {
    System.out.println(" Uploading on Amazone S3 ");
  }
}
```

We have declared an interface called `Cloud`, which will be implemented by each concrete class. The `CloudUpload` class represents a `Context` class. It holds the reference to `Cloud`, which is supplied through a constructor which is as follows:

```
public class CloudUpload {
  private final Cloud cloud;
  public CloudUpload(Cloud cloud) {
    this.cloud = cloud;
  }
  public void upload() {
    this.cloud.upload();
  }
}
```

In this design, each cloud implementation class has the logic of uploading a document to that particular cloud only, obeying the **single responsibility** principle. The `CloudUpload` class does not have a direct reference to any concrete class, but a reference of type `Cloud`, which holds the actual implementation. In this case, we are following this principle: **program to an interface, not implementation**.

After applying the strategy pattern, you may now upload the document by creating an object of the `CloudUpload` class and passing the appropriate implementation in the constructor, as in the following snippet:

```
public class StrategyDemo {
  public static void main(String[] args) {
    CloudUpload googleCloud = new CloudUpload(new GoogleDriveCloud());
    googleCloud.upload();
    CloudUpload dropBpxCloud = new CloudUpload(new DropboxCloud());
    dropBpxCloud.upload();
    CloudUpload oneDriveCloud = new CloudUpload(new OneDriveCloud());
    oneDriveCloud.upload();
    CloudUpload amazoneS3Cloud = new CloudUpload(new AmazoneS3Cloud());
    amazoneS3Cloud.upload();
  }
}
```

In case of additional cloud implementation support in future, there is no change to the `CloudUpload` class. Unit testing becomes straightforward and easy. The `CloudUpload` class simply knows what to do with the strategy classes (the `Cloud` implementation) instead of putting conditional blocks to choose a specific implementation.

This way, the strategy pattern helps us to achieve pluggable behavior. The logic of choosing the `Cloud` implementation is now shifted from the `CloudUpload` class. This is how IoC is achieved with the help of the strategy pattern.

Configuration styles

Almost all IoC containers allow you to choose either code or file-based (XML) configuration for declaring dependencies. Although they serve the same purpose, you might feel confused as to which option is best for the given scenario.

For instance, file-based (mainly XML) configuration is appropriate for the applications that need deployment to multiple environments. On the other hand, there are specific scenarios where code-based configuration is chosen over file-based configuration. Identifying the difference between these two will help you choose which one is right for you.

File-based (XML) versus code-based configuration

The benefit of XML-based configuration is that you can alter dependencies without recompiling, building, and deploying the application code. This sounds useful in a situation where you need to swap the dependencies of the same type. But again, is this really what you are looking for? In other words, if you do not have the requirements for changing the implementation of dependencies on the fly at runtime, then file-based configuration is not that useful.

On the downside, file-based configuration is generally more difficult to read and analyze, especially when it becomes large and clumsy. XML-based configuration does not warn you about any errors at compile time. Such errors can only be picked up at runtime, and they are quite tricky and time-consuming to fix. On the other hand, code-based configuration supports compile-time error checking. This means that if the build is successful, you are done and will not get any surprises at runtime.

Injection using the setter method versus the constructor

There are two straightforward options of DI – setter- or constructor-based DI. Both of these methods perform the same operation—injecting dependencies—but at different times of the object's lifespan. One happens during object instantiation, while the other happens on calling the setter method explicitly.

A very obvious dilemma comes into the picture when you implement DI with these two options. Understanding the difference is important because it reflects the basic problem of the object-oriented programming context: do we initiate the field variable with the constructor argument or through the setter method?

Constructor-based DI

Passing dependencies with a constructor is more clear in terms of describing what is required to create an object. You may write multiple versions of constructors, each taking a different combination of dependency objects, if that is allowed.

Alongside initializing fields with the constructor, you can hide them by not providing a setter method. The advantage of this arrangement is that you can make sure the dependencies being set through the constructor will be available for the lifespan of an object. This is important, because if you do not want a particular dependency to be changed with the birth of an object, then initializing it with the constructor and not providing a setter will make it immutable. A constructor-based DI will decide the DI order while loading the context.

Passing the dependencies through the constructor will manage the order of the object creation graph and will eventually reduce the risk of circular dependency. Conversely, for constructor-based DI, Spring does not allow you to create a proxy with the **Code Generation Library** (CGLIB). You need to use either an interface-based proxy or a no-argument constructor.

You should choose the approach of passing dependencies into a constructor as your default preference. Ideally, all active/mandatory dependencies must be passed through a constructor.

Setter-based DI

The basic idea behind setter-based DI is that once the object is created (mainly with no argument constructors), a setter can be called to supply the dependencies to form an object graph, or just to supply the mock object for testing purposes.

Constructor-based DI is appropriate if there are only a couple of constructor parameters. If there are lots of constructor parameters, it will look messy. Even multiple versions of a constructor will not help much. In this case, you should rely on setter-based DI.

Ideally, all optional or conditional dependencies should be supplied through setter-based DI. The drawback to this approach is that you should make sure the setter methods are called before a client object starts using it. Another risk in using the setter method is that the dependency being altered at a later part of execution will result in an unexpected or ambiguous result, which is sometimes hard to trace. Also, if configuration is not done properly with the setter approach, you may end up with a circular dependency, which you could face at runtime.

Circular dependency

A circular or cyclic dependency is a situation where two or more independent modules or components rely on each other to function properly. This is referred to as mutual recursion. Circular dependency generally occurs in a modular framework while defining a dependency between modules or components.

The term circular dependency is very common across domain models where a set of objects are associated with each other. Circular dependencies between classes are not necessarily harmful. In fact, in particular situations, they are appropriate. Take an example of an application where you are dealing with domain objects such as a student and a course. You probably need a `Student` class that gets courses a student has enrolled in, and a `Course` class that gets a list of students enrolled on that course. It is clear that the `Student` and the `Course` classes are interdependent, but if circular dependency is required in this case, then taking a chance to remove it may introduce some other problems.

In a software design context, circular dependency between software components or modules produces a negative effect and is hence considered a bad practice. This is probably a design issue. Generally, a software design with a poorly managed dependency is harder to maintain than one with a clear and layered module structure. While designing the system in a modular fashion, you need to keep in mind the problems that occur, especially due to circular dependency.

Problems of circular dependency

Circular dependency can create many redundant effects in software programs. The very first among them in terms of design is the tight coupling between mutually dependent modules, which results in reusing an individual module becoming more difficult or impossible. In general, there are several reasons why you should avoid circular references between objects. It creates the following problems:

- **No dependency hierarchy and no reusability:** Generally, we quantify the code with the layer it is at; for example, high level, low level, and so on. Every layer should only set a dependency (if any) on the layers below it. Normally, when you define dependency between modules, a dependency graph or hierarchy will be created, but in the case of a circular dependency situation, this will be eradicated. This means that there is no dependency hierarchy. For example, say you have the following dependency hierarchy:
    - Module A depends on module B

- Module B depends on module C
- Assume that, at present, module C has no dependencies

Based on this arrangement, we can identify module A as the top level, module B as somewhere in the middle level, and module C as the lower level of the hierarchy. Let's say that, after some time, we need to make module C dependent on module A (for whatever reason).

When this happens, there is no more differentiation between the high, middle, and low levels, which means that there is no longer a hierarchy. All modules are at the same level. Also, since they are in a circular dependency, they are no longer independent. This situation forms a single giant virtual module, which is divided into interdependent pieces. You cannot use any of them independently.

- **Changing replication:** Circular dependency creates a ripple effect of changes. For example, if any change happens in one module, this may impact other modules, which results in undesirable effects on the overall software architecture, such as compilation errors, and logical program errors. Due to its nature, circular dependency may create other unpredictable issues, such as endless recursion.
- **Readability and maintainability:** Code that has a circular reference is naturally harder to understand and read than code that doesn't have a circular reference. Such code is intrinsically delicate and easy to breach. Ensuring that your code is free from circular dependencies will make the code easy to work with and make the code be able to accommodate changes with ease, resulting in easy maintenance. From a unit testing point of view, code that has a circular dependency is more difficult to test since it can't be isolated.

Causes and solutions

As we have already seen, circular dependency mostly occurs as a result of bad design/coding practice. In large software application development, the coders may deviate from the context and produce a circular reference.

To overcome this, you can take the help of various tools to find unwanted circular dependencies. This should be an ongoing activity and be applied from the beginning of the development cycle. For example, Eclipse has a plugin called Java Dependency Viewer, which will help to see the dependency between classes and Java packages.

Issues of circular dependency can be addressed by following certain patterns and principles, which are discussed in the following sections.

The single responsibility principle

Let's understand how circular dependency can be eliminated by applying the single responsibility principle. Let's assume you are following three modules in a system:

- Salary module
- Employee module
- HR module

The **Salary module** generates salary and sends it over email. Generating salary depends upon the **Employee module**. To get a few details, such as the appraisal process, and reward points the **Employee module** depends upon the HR module. At this moment, the dependency hierarchy will be as shown in the following diagram:

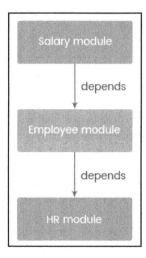

At some point in time, let's say you need email functionality in the **HR module**. Since email functionality is present in the **Salary module**, you decide to give dependency of the **Salary module** to the **HR module**. At this moment, the dependency graph looks like the following diagram:

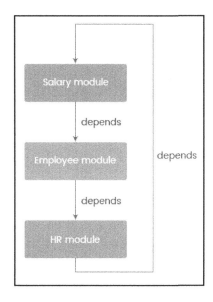

This situation forms a circular dependency. To avoid this, you need to follow the single responsibility principle. This principle states that a module or class should hold responsibility of a single part of the functionality. That module or class should take total ownership of that functionality and must be encapsulated entirely. All services provided by the module must not deviate from the main functionality.

In our case, the Salary module not only generates salary, but sends emails, too. This is a violation of the single responsibility principle. When a single module performs more than one responsibility, there's a chance of poor dependency management, which may result in either:

- **Code duplication:** You may write similar and common functionalities in multiple modules. For example, in this case, you may write an email sending functionality in the HR module to avoid circular dependency, but will end up with code duplication, which raises maintenance problems later on.
- **Circular dependency:** As we have seen in the preceding case.

You need to write a separate module called the Utility module and put the email sending functionality in that. After you have refactored this code, both the **HR module** and the **Salary module** are now dependent on the Utility module. This is how circular dependency can be removed: by following the single responsibility principle.

Deferring the setting of a dependency from constructor to setter

Let's understand how solves circular dependency by providing a dependency from the constructor to the setter method. There is a special case where due to circular dependency, you can't even create the object of the domain model. For example, say you are developing an application for a `tyre` manufacturer; who uses these tyres for cars. Based on the car's max speed, you need to set the min rim size of the `tyre`. For this, you have created the `Car` and `Tyre` classes, as in the following snippet:

```
public class Car {
   private Tyre tyre;
   private int maxSpeed;

   public Car(Tyre tyre) {
      this.tyre = tyre;
      setMaxSpeed(150);
   }
   public int getMaxSpeed() {
      return maxSpeed;
   }
   public void setMaxSpeed(int maxSpeed) {
      this.maxSpeed = maxSpeed;
   }
}


public class Tyre {
   private Car car;
   private int minRimSize;
   public Tyre(Car car) {
      this.car = car;
      if(this.car.getMaxSpeed()>100 && this.car.getMaxSpeed()<200) {
         setMinRimSize(15);
      }else if(this.car.getMaxSpeed()<100) {
         System.out.println("Minimum RIM size is 14");
         setMinRimSize(14);
      }
   }
```

```
   public int getMinRimSize() {
     return minRimSize;
   }
   public void setMinRimSize(int minRimSize) {
     this.minRimSize = minRimSize;
   }
}
```

As you can see, the `Car` and `Tyre` classes are dependent on each another. The dependency is passed through the constructor, hence why it is a circular dependency. You can't create an object for either of them. To handle this situation, you need to defer setting the dependency from the constructor to the setter in each case. We decided to make this change in the `Car` class, as in the following snippet:

```
public class Car{
   private Tyre tyre;
   private int maxSpeed;
   public Car() {
   }
   public void setTyre(Tyre tyre) {
     this.tyre = tyre;
   }
   public Tyre getTyre() {
     return tyre;
   }
   public int getMaxSpeed() {
     return maxSpeed;
   }
   public void setMaxSpeed(int maxSpeed) {
     this.maxSpeed = maxSpeed;
   }
}
```

The dependency (of `Tyre`) is moved from the constructor to the setter method. In the `Tyre` class, you need to set a reference of the current class (`Tyre`) into the `Car` object, as in the following snippet:

```
public class Tyre {

   private Car car;
   private int minRimSize;
   public Tyre(Car car) {
     this.car = car;
     this.car.setTyre(this);
     if(this.car.getMaxSpeed()>100 && this.car.getMaxSpeed()<200) {
       System.out.println("Minimum RIM size is 15");
       setMinRimSize(15);
```

```
      }else if(this.car.getMaxSpeed()<100) {
        System.out.println("Minimum RIM size is 14");
        setMinRimSize(14);
      }
    }
  public int getMinRimSize() {
    return minRimSize;
  }
  public void setMinRimSize(int minRimSize) {
    this.minRimSize = minRimSize;
  }
}
```

Everything is settled now. You can create an object of type `Car` first, then create an object of type `Tyre` so that you can pass the reference of the `car` object to it. The client code will be as in the following code snippet:

```
public class CircularDependencyWithSetterDemo {

  public static void main(String[] args) {
      Car car = new Car();
      car.setMaxSpeed(120);
      Tyre tyre = new Tyre(car);
      car.setMaxSpeed(90);
      tyre = new Tyre(car);
  }
}
```

Relocation of classes and packages

One of the possible reasons for circular dependency is a chain of dependencies starting from some classes in a Java package. Let's say that `com.packt.util` traverses with a different package and reaches some other class in the same package, `com.packt.util`. This is a package arrangement issue that can be solved by moving the classes and restructuring the packages. You can perform such refactoring activities with modern IDEs.

Circular dependency in the Spring framework

Let's explore how circular dependency occurs in the Spring framework and how to deal with it. Spring provides an IoC container that loads all the beans and tries to create objects in a specific order so that they work properly. For example, say we have three beans with the following dependency hierarchy:

- `Employee` bean
- `HRService` bean
- `CommonUtilService` bean

The `Employee` bean depends on the `HRService` bean, which depends on the `CommonUtilService` bean.

In this case, `CommonUtilService` is considered a low-level bean, while the Employee bean is considered a high-level bean. Spring will first create an object for all low-level beans so that it creates the `CommonUtilService` bean, then it will create the `HRService` bean (and inject the object of the `CommonUtilService` bean into it), and then it will create an object of the `Employee` bean (and inject the object of the `HRService` bean into it).

Now, you need to make the `CommonUtilService` bean dependent on the `Employee`. This is circular dependency. Furthermore, all dependencies are set through a constructor.

In the case of circular dependency, the difference between high and low-level modules disappears. This means that Spring will be in a dilemma of which bean should be instantiated first, since they depend on each other. As a result, Spring will raise a `BeanCurrentlyInCreationException` error.

 This will only happen in the case of constructor injection. If dependencies are set through the setter method, this problem will not occur, even if beans are interdependent. This is because at the time of context loading, no dependencies are present.

Let's create the code for this and see how Spring detects circular dependency. The code will be as follows:

```
@Component("commonUtilService")
public class CommonUtilService {
  private Employee employee;
  public CommonUtilService(Employee employee) {
    this.employee = employee;
  }
}
```

```
@Component("employee")
public class Employee {
  private HRService hrService;
  public Employee(HRService hrService) {
    this.hrService=hrService;
  }
}

@Component("hrService")
public class HRService {
  private CommonUtilService commonUtilService;
  public HRService(CommonUtilService commonUtilService) {
    this.commonUtilService=commonUtilService;
  }
}
```

The Java config and client code will be as in the following snippet:

```
@Configuration
@ComponentScan(basePackages="com.packt.spring.circulardependency.model.simp
le")
public class SpringConfig {
}

public class SpringCircularDependencyDemo {
  public static void main(String[] args) {
    ApplicationContext springContext = new
AnnotationConfigApplicationContext(SpringConfig.class);
    Employee employee = (Employee) springContext.getBean("employee");
    HRService hrService = (HRService) springContext.getBean("hrService");
    CommonUtilService commonUtilService = (CommonUtilService)
springContext.getBean("commonUtilService");
  }
}
```

On running this code, you will get a `BeanCurrentlyInCreationException` error for all the beans, as follows:

```
Unsatisfied dependency expressed through constructor parameter 0; nested
exception is
org.springframework.beans.factory.UnsatisfiedDependencyException: Error
creating bean with name 'employee' defined in file
```

To avoid this situation, you need to redesign the preceding structure. In a few circumstances, it's not possible to change the structure, maybe due to design limitations of the legacy code. In this case, Spring provides some solutions, as follows.

Using setter/field injection over constructor injection

This is probably the most easy and straightforward option. In circular dependency, if constructor injection creates a circular reference, you can defer the DI in the setter method. This allows Spring to load a bean context without any issues. The updated code would be as follows:

```
@Component("employee")
public class Employee {
  private HRService hrService;
  @Autowired
  public void setHrService(HRService hrService) {
    this.hrService = hrService;
    System.out.println(" HRService dependency is set ");
  }
}

@Component("hrService")
public class HRService {
  private CommonUtilService commonUtilService;
  @Autowired
  public void setCommonUtilService(CommonUtilService commonUtilService) {
    this.commonUtilService = commonUtilService;
    System.out.println(" CommonUtilService dependency is set ");
  }
}

@Component("commonUtilService")
public class CommonUtilService {
  private Employee employee;
  @Autowired
  public void setEmployee(Employee employee) {
    this.employee = employee;
    System.out.println(" Employee dependency is set ");
  }
}
```

All dependencies are set in the setter method with the @Autowired annotation. Spring will create instances of all three beans first and will then set them with the setter method.

 Setting the @Autowired annotation on fields of the bean is equivalent to setter injection. If you annotate the fields of the class with the @Autowired annotation, Spring will not complain about circular dependency.

Using the @Lazy annotation

Another workaround is to use the @Lazy annotation. This annotation will instruct Spring to load the bean only when it is used, instead of at the time of context loading. Spring will create a proxy of the bean during context loading and will pass it into another object. The updated code will look as follows:

```
@Component("employee")
public class Employee {
  private HRService hrService;
  public Employee(@Lazy HRService hrService) {
    this.hrService=hrService;
  }
  public void displayEmployeeName() {
    System.out.println(" Employee name is Nilang ");
  }
}

@Component("hrService")
public class HRService {
  private CommonUtilService commonUtilService;
  public HRService(@Lazy CommonUtilService commonUtilService) {
    this.commonUtilService=commonUtilService;
  }
}

@Component("commonUtilService")
public class CommonUtilService {
  private Employee employee;
  public CommonUtilService(@Lazy Employee employee) {
    this.employee = employee;
  }
  public void showEmployeeNameFromDependency() {
    this.employee.displayEmployeeName();
  }
}
```

The constructor dependencies are set through the @Lazy annotation. This code will run without any issue. The actual dependency is injected only when it's being called. To demonstrate this, the displayEmployeeName method is created in the Employee bean, which we will call with the dependency reference from the CommonUtilService bean, as in the following snippet:

```
ApplicationContext springContext = new
AnnotationConfigApplicationContext(SpringConfigForLazy.class);
    Employee employee = (Employee) springContext.getBean("employee");
    HRService hrService = (HRService) springContext.getBean("hrService");
```

```
      CommonUtilService commonUtilService = (CommonUtilService)
  springContext.getBean("commonUtilService");
      commonUtilService.showEmployeeNameFromDependency();
```

When the `showEmployeeNameFromDependency` method is called, it will internally call the `displayEmployeeName` method on the employee reference in `CommonUtilService`. When this happens, Spring will actually inject the dependency. You will get the following output:

```
  Employee name is Nilang
```

Best practices and anti-patterns

So far, we have talked about using IoC containers to achieve DI, but one of the most common mistakes is to use IoC containers without doing real DI. This may sound strange, but it is a fact. Such mistakes are possible in the absence of having a proper understanding of underlying concepts.

Ideally, DI implementation should only reference the IoC container during the time of the application's startup. If a developer wraps the IoC container itself and passes it into other component to reduce any dependency, this is not a good design. Let's understand this issue with an example.

What to inject – the container itself or just dependencies?

The situation of injecting container occurs when you try to wrap the container itself either in a singleton class or a public static method to provide the dependency to other components or modules, as in the following snippet:

```
public class AccountService {
  //Service method.
  public void getVariablePay() {
    System.out.println("getting variable pay..");
  }
}

public class HRService {
  public int getLeaveInGivenMonth(int monthNo) {
    System.out.println(" getting no of leaves for month "+monthNo);
    return 2; // just for demo purpose.
  }
```

```
}
/* ServiceManager serves like dependency supplier */
public class ServiceManager {
  private static ApplicationContext springContext = new
ClassPathXmlApplicationContext("application-context.xml");
 private ServiceManager() {
  }
  //This method will return the dependency
  public static Object getDependentService(String serviceName) {
    Object dependency = null;
    if(springContext !=null) {
      dependency = springContext.getBean(serviceName);
    }
    return dependency;
  }
}

public class EmployeeService {
  private AccountService accountService;
  private HRService hrService;
  //constructor
  public EmployeeService() {
    if(ServiceManager.getDependentService("accountService") !=null) {
      accountService = (AccountService)
ServiceManager.getDependentService("accountService");
    }
    if(ServiceManager.getDependentService("hrService") !=null) {
      hrService = (HRService)
ServiceManager.getDependentService("hrService");
    }
  }
  public void generateRewardPoints() {
    if(hrService !=null && accountService !=null) {
      int noOfLeaves = this.hrService.getLeaveInGivenMonth(8);
      System.out.println("No of Leaves are : "+noOfLeaves);
      this.accountService.getVariablePay();
      //Some complex logic to generate rewards points based on variable
pay and total leave
      //taken in given month.
    }
  }
}
```

This is equivalent to the service locator pattern. In this code, the `ServiceManager` class holds the reference of the container. It will return the dependency (services) through its static method. The `EmployeeService` class uses the `ServiceManager` to get its dependencies (`HRService` and `AccountService`). At first glance, this looks perfectly fine as we don't want the `EmployeeService` to be tightly coupled with `HRService` and `AccountService`.

Though we removed the coupling of dependencies in the preceding code, this is not what we mean by DI. The fundamental mistake in the preceding case is that instead of providing the dependency, we are relying on other classes to supply it. In reality, we are removing the dependency of one entity, but adding another. This is one of the classic examples of using an IoC container very badly and without implementing DI properly.

The `ServiceManager` class is a singleton class that supplies the dependencies with its static method. Instead of injecting `HRService` and `AccountService` into `EmployeeService`, we are relying on `SerivceManager` to provide the dependency.

You might argue that the preceding approach will replace multiple dependencies with a single class, and will effectively reduce the dependency. However, the benefits of DI are not 100% achieved. The design issue of being tightly dependent on `ServiceManager` is unseen until any change happens in that class. For example, if you change the configuration of either the `HRManager` or `AccoutService` class, you need to change the code of `ServiceManager`.

Another side effect of this scenario is that things are not clear from a unit testing point of view. The benefit of DI is that just by looking at the constructor of the class, you should know what things are dependent on it so that you can inject the mock object very easily while doing unit testing.

The scenario in this case is the opposite. Ideally, the caller should supply the dependency, but in our case, the caller doesn't provide anything, while the component (`EmployeeService`) is getting the dependencies by using its own singleton class. The constructor of the `EmployeeService` class will be empty and you probably won't determine its dependency until you refer to its source code thoroughly.

The preceding design is more of a service locator implementation. However, there are a few other limitations of the service locator, as follows:

- **Isolation:** The services added into the registry are ultimately black boxes to the caller or client class. This results in a less reliable system as it would be difficult to identify and rectify the errors that occur in the dependency services.

- **Concurrency:** The service locator has a unique registry of services, which may cause a performance bottleneck if it is accessed by concurrent components.
- **Dependency resolution:** For the client code, the registry provided by the service locator is kind of a black box, and this may cause issues at runtime, for example, if dependencies are not yet registered, or there are any dependency-specific issues.
- **Maintainability:** In the service locator, since the code of the service implementation is isolated from clients, it is unclear when the new changes will break this functionality at runtime.
- **Testability:** The service locator stores all of the services in the registry, which makes unit testing a bit harder since all of the tests may rely on the registry to set various mock service classes explicitly.

Our goal is to make the client code 100% decoupled from its dependencies or any class who supplies the dependencies. In the preceding case, we want to break the coupling between `EmployeeService` and its dependencies.

Let's improve the preceding design and rewrite the `EmployeeSerice` class, as in the following snippet:

```
public class EmployeeService {
    private AccountService accountService;
    private HRService hrService;
    //constructor
    public EmployeeService(AccountService accountService,HRService hrService)
    {
        this.accountService = accountService;
        this.hrService = hrService;
    }
    public void generateRewardPoints() {
        if(hrService !=null && accountService !=null) {
            int noOfLeaves = this.hrService.getLeaveInGivenMonth(8);
            System.out.println("No of Leaves are : "+noOfLeaves);
            this.accountService.getVariablePay();
            //Some complex logic to generate rewards points based on variable pay
and total leave
            //taken in given month.
        }
    }
}
```

Now, the `EmployeeService` class does not depend on
the `HRService` and `AccountService` classes. This is what we wanted to achieve. Your
business code should not know anything about its dependencies. It is the IoC container's job
to provide them. This code is now more readable and easy to understand. The
dependencies can be predicated just by looking at the constructor.

If you wish to instantiate `EmployeeService`, you just need to pass the object of
the `HRService` and `AccountService` classes. While doing unit testing, you can just pass
the mock objects and test the integration between these services. The process becomes very
simple now. This is the correct implementation and meaning of DI.

Excessive injection

Every design pattern solves specific design problems, but any single pattern is not
necessarily appropriate for every case that you come across. A pattern or methodology you
are applying should be chosen because it is the right choice for the given problem, not just
because you know it and wish to implement it.

Dependency injection is a pattern (and not a framework), so you need to consider the right
scenario to implement it. There are chances that may make DI become redundant. It is not
necessary to inject everything in your code. If you do so, the purpose of making the code
decoupled is not achieved properly; instead, the dependency graph becomes ineffectual.

Evidently, DI produces great flexibility in terms of code maintenance, executing unit testing
in a more meaningful and useful way to achieve modularity. However, you should utilize
its flexibility only when you really need to. The intention of DI is to diminish coupling
instead of wrapping and supplying every single dependency, which is not a wise decision.

For example, let's say that you need a `Calendar` object to perform various calendar-related
operations. The traditional way is by using a static method - `getInstance` of the `Calendar`
class, for example, `Calendar.getInstance()`. It is a kind of static factory within
the `Calendar` class, which creates the object.

If you try to pass the `Calendar` object with DI, you will not achieve anything new. All of the methods in which the `Calendar` object is passed through (an entire call chain – from where it is injected to where it is used) will have additional arguments. This ultimately adds the burden of passing the `Calendar` object to the programmer. Also, the `Calendar` object is not injected with an abstraction, so the argument is of the `Calendar` type rather than any abstract or interface. This means that there is no clear benefit of changing the implementation because we are passing the dependency with the concrete type rather than the abstract type (because that is not possible for the `Calendar` class in Java).

Ideally, any Java, third library, or custom class that simply provides static functionality that can be common across all components or modules should be used either statically (class reference) or in a single instance mechanism (if an instance is required) instead of injecting them into classes.

Another example is using `Logger` in Java. A typical way of getting a logger instance is to call the `getLogger` static method of the `Logger` class and pass the class which you want to provide the logging feature of. In this case, passing the `Logger` object with DI would be overkill.

Not only that, but injecting such a library with DI would result in reducing the availability of functionalities available only to those components that take the dependencies either through a constructor, the method, or property injection. Also, there is almost no chance of providing any meaningful abstraction that can be easily applied to any such libraries. This will keep you from getting any meaningful flexibility over the implementation.

Choose DI patterns when you need to supply dependencies with different configurations of dependencies or when you want to back different implementations of the same dependency. If it is not required to mix up your dependencies or to supply different implementations, then DI is not an appropriate solution.

Achieving IoC in the absence of a container

Now, we are well aware that DI is meant to provide the dependencies to components through either a constructor, the setter method, or properties to make them separate from dependency services. The conventional understanding is that this can only be possible by using IoC containers. However, this is not true for all cases.

Ideally, IoC containers should be used for configuring and resolving a comparatively large set of dependencies in complex applications. If you are dealing with a simple application that has just a few components and dependencies, it is sensible not to use containers. Instead, you can wire dependencies manually.

Also, in the case of any legacy system where the integration of a container is difficult, you can opt for supplying dependencies manually. You can implement various patterns, such as the factory method, service locator, strategy, or template method patterns, to manage the dependencies.

Summary

We have learned a few important points about the best practices and patterns for managing dependencies in this chapter. Though it is proven that DI brings greater flexibility and modularity in the code by decoupling the client code from its dependencies, there are a few things that we should follow to get the best out of it.

In the beginning, we learned about patterns other than DI that help us to implement IoC. You can definitely use them in your code to decouple modules where the use of IoC containers is not possible. For example, in a legacy code where managing dependencies is not possible through an IoC container, these patterns are useful to achieve IoC.

We became familiar with various configuration options and learned how to choose the right one. We also saw the injection styles used in wiring the dependencies. When working with dependency management, one very obvious problem that occurs is circular reference, which causes circular dependency. We have observed what problems circular dependencies create, what the cause of them is, and how to avoid them in coding.

At the end, we dived into best practices, patterns, and anti-patterns that you should follow while using DI. If we know how to do something, it does not mean that it is applicable all the time. The same is applicable to DI. It is a pattern, and hence it should be used in the right manner to solve specific problems. It may not be suitable for all conditions.

We are taking a pause here. We hope you enjoyed the journey of learning about DI throughout the book. We tried to convey the fundamentals as simply as possible.

Other Books You May Enjoy

If you enjoyed this book, you may be interested in these other books by Packt:

Java 9 Cookbook
Mohamed Sanaulla, Nick Samoylov

ISBN: 978-1-78646-873-4

- Set up JDK and know the differences in the JDK 9 installation
- Implement OO Designs using Classes and Interfaces
- Manage operating system processes
- Understand the new modular JDK and modular programming
- Create a modular application with clear dependencies
- Build graphical user interfaces using JavaFX
- Use the new HTTP Client API
- Learn about the new diagnostic features in Java 9
- See how to use the new jShell REPL tool
- Execute ES6-compliant JavaScript code from your Java applications

Mastering Java 9
Dr. Edward Lavieri, Peter Verhas

ISBN: 978-1-78646-140-7

- Write modular Java applications in terms of the newly introduced module system
- Migrate existing Java applications to modular ones
- Understand how to use the G1 garbage collector in order to leverage the performance of your applications
- Leverage the possibilities provided the newly introduced Java shell
- Test your application's effectiveness with the JVM harness
- See how Java 9 provides support for the http 2.0 standard
- Use the new process API
- Discover additional enhancements and features provided by Java 9

Leave a review - let other readers know what you think

Please share your thoughts on this book with others by leaving a review on the site that you bought it from. If you purchased the book from Amazon, please leave us an honest review on this book's Amazon page. This is vital so that other potential readers can see and use your unbiased opinion to make purchasing decisions, we can understand what our customers think about our products, and our authors can see your feedback on the title that they have worked with Packt to create. It will only take a few minutes of your time, but is valuable to other potential customers, our authors, and Packt. Thank you!

Index

XML metadata configuration 134
bean
  about 178
  autowiring mode 126
  class 126
  constructor-arg 126
  destruction method 126
  initialization method 126
  lazy initialization mode 126
  name 126
  properties 126
bindings, Google Guice framework
  annotations 119
  built-in bindings 118
  constructor bindings 117
  instance bindings 117
  Just-in-time (JIT) binding 119
  linked bindings 116
  untargeted bindings 117
built-in bindings
  Loggers 118

C

circular dependency
  about 207
  causes and solutions 208
  classes and packages, reloacation 213
  dependency setting, differences 211
  in Spring framework 214
  issues 207
  single responsibility principle, using 209
command line interface
  used, for writing modular code 50
configuration styles
  about 204
  file-based (XML), versus code-based 205
constructor bindings 117
constructor injection 121
constructor-based DI 67, 71
Context Dependency Injection (CDI) 27

D

Dependency Injection (DI), Google Guice
  field injection 122

method injection 122
optional injection 122
static injection 123
Dependency Injection (DI), Spring
  about 66
  and bean scope 148
  constructor-based DI 67, 70
  factory method, using 73
  setter-based DI 71
Dependency Injection (DI)
  about 5, 22
  and bean scope 140, 143
  constructor injection 22, 121
  example 102
  interface injection 24
  Modular Framework, using 46
  setter injection 23
  setter-based DI 206
  types 22
  using, with Java configuration 93, 95
Dependency Injection Principle (DIP)
  about 5
  implementing, through IoC 12
Dependency Inversion Principle (DIP) 7, 11, 188
design patterns
  about 5, 6
  advantages 6
design principle 6
DIP implementation, through IoC
  interface, inverting 12, 15
  object creation, inversion through factory pattern 19
  object creation, inversion through service locator 21
  object creation, inverting 15, 17
  object creation, inverting ways 19

E

excessive injection 222
Expression Language (EL) 59

F

factory method pattern
  concrete implementation 190, 191, 193
  creator interface 191

Made in the USA
Coppell, TX
15 November 2020